NEWPORT
The Artful City

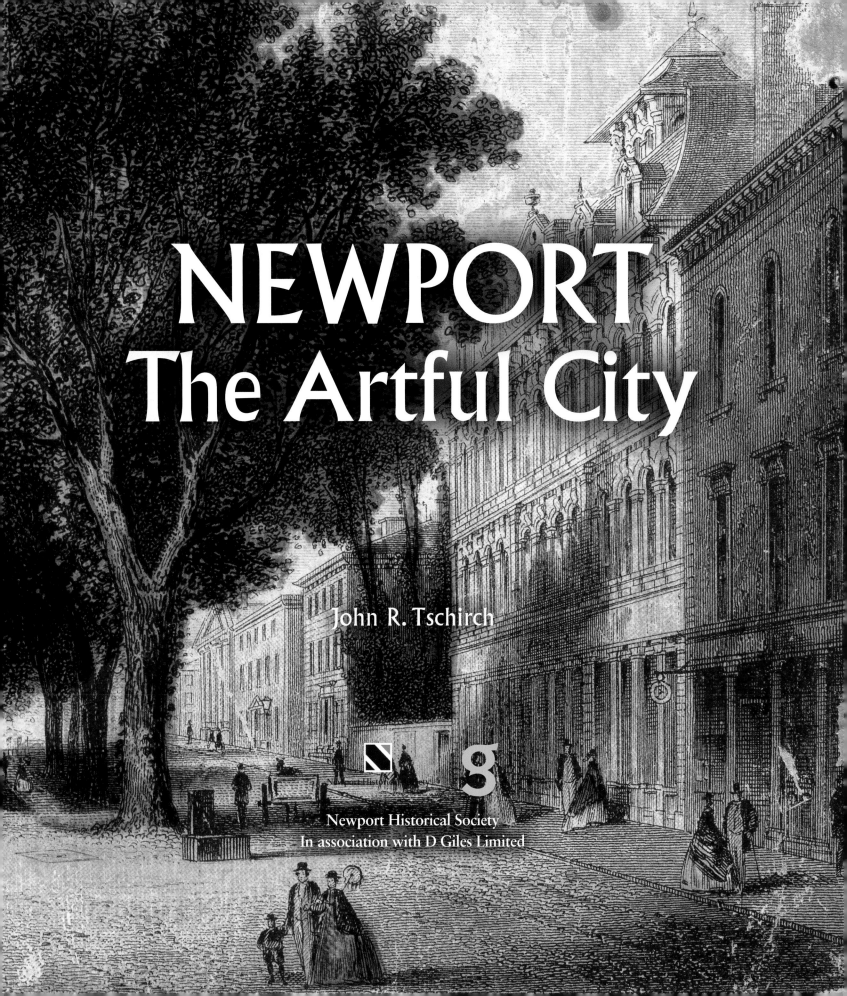

NEWPORT
The Artful City

John R. Tschirch

Newport Historical Society
In association with D Giles Limited

This volume was completed under the aegis of the Newport Historical Society with the support of the EJMP Fund for Philanthropy.

© 2020 The Newport Historical Society and John R. Tschirch

First published in 2020 by GILES
An imprint of D Giles Limited
66 High Street
Lewes, BN7 1XG, UK
gilesltd.com

ISBN: 978-1-911282-69-3

For the Newport Historical Society:
Executive Director: Ruth S. Taylor
Project Director: John R. Tschirch
Photograph Editor: Kaela Bleho

For D Giles Limited:
Copyedited and proofread by Magda Nakassis
Designed by Matthew Wilson
Produced by GILES, an imprint of D Giles Limited
Printed and bound in China

Front cover

Frederick Childe Hassam, *October Sundown*, Newport (1901). Overlay: L.2017.001, *Map of the Township of Newport* (1860), on loan to the Newport Historical Society from Anne Hamilton.

Back cover

Colony House at the eastern end of Washington Square, ca. 1885, photograph. Newport Historical Society, P8620.

Frontispiece

View of Washington Square, ca. 1860, print. Newport Historical Society, FIC.2013.38.

Dedication

THIS BOOK IS DEDICATED TO THE GENERATIONS who have kept Newport's history alive through their generous donations of documents, works of art, objects of historic interest, and financial support to the Newport Historical Society. Dr. David King Jr., a physician, world traveler, and founder of the Newport Historical Society in 1854, is a prominent example of an individual who saw Newport's significance both in terms of its rich past and the promise of its future.

The author, John R. Tschirch, has a remarkably original approach to exploring Newport's historical evolution through its urban plan; in its streets, public spaces, and buildings; in maps; and in the works of those painters, poets, and photographers who saw the beauty and significance of this city as a work of art. In John's words, "this book could not happen without the rich collections and archives of the Newport Historical Society, which distills over three centuries of the city's development."

Elizabeth "Lisette" Prince
Trustee, EJMP Fund for Philanthropy

CONTENTS

FOREWORD

This volume is the result of a shared fascination with the city of Newport. Its illustrious and complicated history, profoundly beautiful natural setting, and abundant survival of the historic built environment result in something magnetic and compelling. We who live and work here see this every day: guests overstay, tourists become residents, and visitors from more than a dozen countries across the globe visit the Newport Historical Society's website to learn more about the city.

Conversations which developed among NHS staff, Elizabeth "Lisette" Prince, and the author John R. Tschirch about maps, historic preservation, and the documented appeal of the city to visitors, even those who will never visit a museum or historic site, coalesced into an idea for a project—something like a visual time line. This book is the evolutionary end point of that project, which also includes a web presence: mappingnewport.org.

The mission of the NHS—to chronicle and interpret Newport's history for a broad audience, so that knowledge of our past will contribute to a deeper understanding of the present and better preparation for the future—has been enhanced by the creation of this work. We are grateful to the scholars who contributed essays that expand and augment the main text, allowing us to tell a more complete and nuanced story.

Finally, it is important to note that Lisette Prince supported this work in all the best ways, from the intellectual to the fiscal. Her love for Newport combined with a newspaperwoman's interest in the facts and a photographer's eye for beauty and detail make her a formidable advocate for this city as both an "accidental work of urban art" and a dynamic living entity. We are extremely grateful for her participation.

Ruth S. Taylor
Executive Director
Newport Historical Society

Opposite

One of the earliest known daguerreotypes of Newport, depicting an aerial view of the Stone Tower in Touro Park looking northwest over the city, ca. 1840, daguerreotype. Newport Historical Society, P9362.

ACKNOWLEDGMENTS

I FIRST ENVISIONED WHAT WOULD BECOME *Newport: The Artful City* while standing in the mud on a rainy day in early spring with Elizabeth "Lisette" Prince, who asked me what I would truly be interested in working on with regard to Newport's heritage. Surrounded by trees beginning to bud and grand houses lining Bellevue Avenue, I said, "the city as an urban work of art." I had been working for years on individual landmark designations, house museum collections, and the stories of various historical figures, all important in their own way, but I was ready to consider the whole place, Newport in its entirety, or, more accurately, my perspective on a city that is so richly layered with history. I thank Lisette for her vision, creativity and commitment to looking at Newport in so many different ways. Without her support, this project would never have come to fruition and been so carefully nurtured along the way.

Ruth Taylor, Executive Director of the Newport Historical Society, has been an extraordinary colleague and collaborator, seeing both the current need and future potential of exploring the city's history from different vantage points. The staff of the Newport Historical Society has also been a pleasure to work with, specifically Kaela Bleho, who did such detailed work on the organization of photographs and archival materials for the book. Thanks also to Bert Lippincott for his insights into the city and rare documents that enriched my story. Molly Bruce Patterson and Sarah Long, both formerly of the Newport Historical Society, committed their time and talents in the first years of my research and conceptual development of *Newport: The Artful City*.

I appreciate the generosity of The Redwood Library and Athenaeum and the Preservation Society of Newport County for their permissions to use their collections.

Thank you also to all future readers of this book. May it bring you entertainment and enrichment.

John R. Tschirch

PREFACE

How does the urban fabric of Newport reflect the cultural conditions that shaped the city? How are artistic, social, political, religious, and economic ideas embedded in streets, buildings, and open spaces? How have both residents and visitors throughout the ages perceived and been affected by their environment as reflected in their artistic production and visual descriptions of the place?

Newport: The Artful City seeks the answers to these questions in an analysis of Newport's physical and cultural development. Architectural history, urban planning, art history, and literature all provide frameworks for the study of a city renowned for the rarity, authenticity, integrity, and national significance of its built heritage.

Through the use of maps, paintings, illustrations, photographs, and literary descriptions, this book charts the physical layout of Newport's streetscapes and the cultural responses the city has inspired for over three and a half centuries of urban development.

I had been enthralled by the great Schliemann's discovery of the site of ancient Troy—those nine cities one on top of the other ... I found—or thought I found—that Newport, Rhode Island, presented nine cities, some superimposed, some having very little relation with the others—variously beautiful, impressive, absurd, commonplace, and one very nearly squalid.

Thornton Wilder
Theophilus North, 1973

INTRODUCTION
The Artful City

Fig. 1

Matthew Dripps, *Map of Newport & vicinity, Rhode Island* (detail), ca. 1870. Library of Congress.

The key character-defining features of Newport's historic urban plan are fully recorded in this map, which displays the main thoroughfare of Thames Street along the harbor and the grid plan of the Point established by European colonists in the seventeenth and early eighteenth centuries; the axial layout of Bellevue Avenue (1853) and the subdivision of farmlands to its east and west; and the serpentine form of Ocean Drive (1867) in the southern portion of the city.

NEWPORT, RHODE ISLAND, IS A PLACE OF MEMORY, both collective and individual, where myth and reality intersect in streets and public spaces. Spectacular scenery, a centuries-old architectural heritage, and the cultural legacy of its residents and visitors make for a storied past. From European settlement in the seventeenth century through the present day, Newport's urban layout has been formed by natural features, such as topography, freshwater sources, and the sea, and the economic, religious, political, and social values of its inhabitants. Through maps, paintings, illustrations, photographs, and literary descriptions, the city's evolution may be traced from the entrepreneurship and religious circumstances determining its colonial streetscapes to the picturesque ideals that inspired the nineteenth-century resort area and the tenets of urban renewal and historic preservation that shaped the twentieth-century city (Fig. 1). Today, in the twenty-first century, Newport is a remarkably intact historic city. Its streets and buildings may be read as lessons from the past, instructions for the present, and revelations of the future.

The distinct physical characteristics of cities and their cultural identity have been inextricably linked. Through literature and the arts, urban entities are often elevated to mythic status, reflecting both the realities and aspirations of an epoch, or epochs, enshrined as a golden age. These complex environments offer many stories through many layers of building, as expressed by urban historian Wolfgang Braunfels:

History tries to encompass overlapping processes. It has to take every aspect of life into consideration. Cities can be understood neither from their beginnings alone nor from their final state. ... Old views of a town complete our knowledge by making circumstances visible to us. What is handed down to us visually teaches us with greater precision about the genesis of buildings, their aesthetic, ideological and semantic rank. ... Cities do not merely report their history ... cities provide the motives for the building of every house and every street. ... We are received by the past whenever we set foot in an old city square, and at the same time we are taught about a past that never denies its ideals in the face of the present.[1]

Newport's various districts distill significant aspects of the history of urban design in America. The colonial quarter's system of wharves is a testament to the economic impetus that formed the city, while the grid established by the Society of Friends on the Point is an example of rational planning dating back to ancient times. The formality of Bellevue Avenue, the picturesque plan of Ocean Drive, and the modern urban renewal features of America's Cup Avenue each reveal aesthetic and commercial forces that have shaped the city through the ages.

Documents of the past, including maps, paintings, illustrations, photographs, and literary accounts, record both the urban evolution of Newport and the creation of its mystique as a historic place, an intangible quality that can be as powerful in its influence over time as the built environment. For how does a storied city become so? How does a mythic place arise? Myths are invented by the human mind, beginning with the land, the sea, the ways in which people make their mark on the topography, and the legends that emerge by those who celebrate the place as time goes by. The physical and the metaphysical combine to make the mythic image.

Upon returning to the United States in 1906, after decades of living abroad, writer Henry James bore witness to both a Newport and a country at large that had greatly changed since the days of his youth. Casting a discerning eye about the city, where he had memories of spending summers with his family, he recorded the empirical evidence of streets, buildings, and scenery and also sought to articulate his feelings about a more mutable, hard to capture, atmosphere as he wrote, "Newport, on my finding myself back there, threatened me sharply, quite at first, with that predicament at which I have glanced in another connection or two—the felt condition of having known it too well and loved it too much for description or definition."[2] Although he confessed his struggle to properly express his sense of the place, James did so with nuance and depth. The writer imagined introducing an observer to the city as a device for explaining the varied aspects of the urban scene and the changing moods that affected him so poignantly in his wanderings as he dwelt upon the presence of history while engaging in the present:

It had been certain ... that he would find the whole picture overpainted, and the question could only be, at the best, of how much of the ancient surface would here and there glimmer through. The ancient surface had been the concern ... of a small minority, the comparatively few people for whom the lurking shy charm, all there, but all to be felt rather than published, did in fact constitute a surface. The question, as soon as one arrived, was of whether some ghosts of that were unrecoverable.[3]

James paints a picture of Newport in prose, creating a richly layered composition of buildings, streets, and historical figures who, if one looked and listened, called out as characters from the past. The interplay of the old and the new evident in James's musings infused the work of so many artists before and since who have encountered the city (Fig. 2). These individuals invariably celebrated and critiqued what can be categorized as an accidental work of urban art, for Newport was never subject to a grand plan with a grand vision. The city is the sum total of centuries of evolution, resulting in a work of art, eliciting many of the responses associated with a work of art: admiration; condemnation; interpretation; and, not least of all, inspiration.

Fig. 2

Raymond Crawford Ewer, "A Sketch-Book at Newport: What a Puck Artist Saw at Society's Summer Capital" (detail), *Puck Magazine* 75, no. 1949 (July 11, 1914). Library of Congress.

An illustration of the social and architectural scenery in Newport, Rhode Island, this rare image captures the whirl of ladies and gentlemen standing before the Newport Casino, yachts in the harbor, and the smart set motoring by the timeworn buildings of the colonial quarter, focusing on the contrast between old and new.

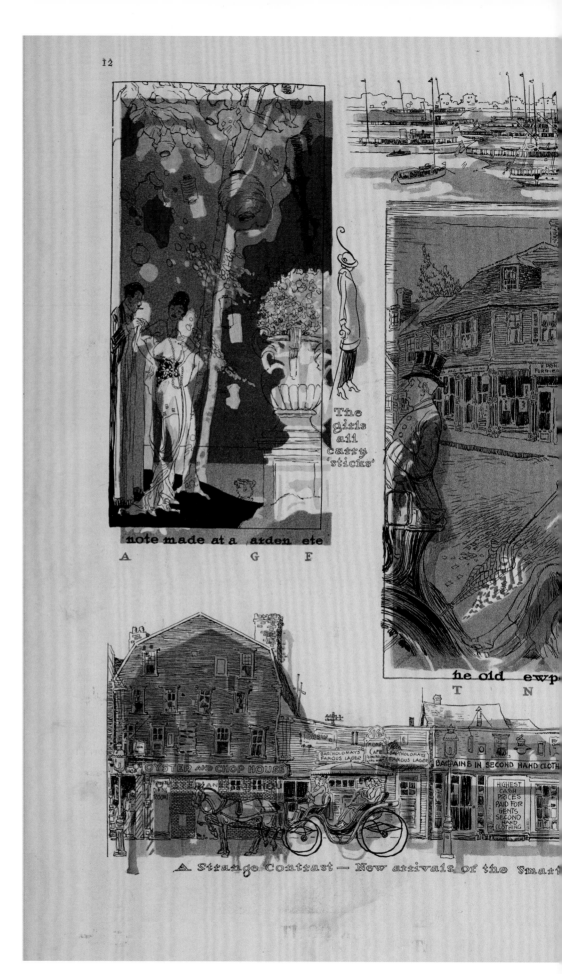

few million dollars worth of yachts in the harbor

CARLO PIERLO CIGARS CANDY

H. ADAM Grocer

the new

An old fashioned New England lady shops while her aristocratic sister awaits her turn

chatting in front of the Casino

One of the Mansions at night

ving up Long Wharf

Most of the ladies of the younger set own and drive powerful cars

RAYMOND CRAWFORD EWER NEWPORT R.I. 04

DRAWN BY RAYMOND C. EWER

KETCH-BOOK AT NEWPORT

uck Artist Saw at Society's Summer Capital

CHAPTER 1

THE OLD QUARTER

Washington Square, Thames Street, and Historic Hill

Foundations

Upon encountering Aquidneck Island in 1524, Giovanni da Verrazzano beheld not a wilderness, but a land marked by human settlement. The Italian sea captain in the service of the French crown was on an expedition to the eastern coastline of North America. He sailed into what would become known as Newport harbor, which he called "Port di Refugio," recording his observations of the topography and its inhabitants in a letter to His Majesty, King Francis I.[4] Although da Verrazzano did not remain long in Narragansett Bay and among its islands, he left behind a written account of the open meadows, cultivated fields, and clusters of dwellings, testifying to an established Native American community with a purposeful use of natural resources.

Another century would pass before Europeans established a permanent presence in the area. In 1639, William Coddington, William Brenton, John Clarke,

We reached a land … where we found an excellent harbor. … When we went farther inland, we saw their houses, which are circular in shape, about XIII to XV paces across, made of bent saplings, they are arranged without any architectural pattern. … They move these houses from one place to another according to the richness of the site and the season.

Giovanni da Verrazzano
Letter to His Majesty, King Francis I, 1524

Previous spread

Samuel King, A Southwest View of Newport, 1795,
engraving. Newport Historical Society, 91.35.1.

Jeremy Clarke, Nicholas Easton, John Coggeshall, Thomas Hazard, Henry Bull, and William Dyer purchased the right from the native Narragansetts to found a settlement on Aquidneck Island:

> *By us whose Hands are underwritten to propagate a Plantation in the midst of the Island or Elsewhere and doe engage ourselves to brave equal charges answerable to our Strength & Estates in Common and that our determination shall be by major voice of Judge and Elders the Judge to have a double voice.*[5]

The language of the agreement affirmed the principles of organization and accountability that governed the founders' actions. This is reinforced by the documented process for deciding upon location, land division, and the choice of a proper name:

> *It is agreed that the Plantation now begun at the South west end of the island shall be called Newport … and that the Towne shall be built upon both sides of the spring, and by the sea Southward.*[6]

The pursuit of personal liberties and the primacy of geographic realities both played their parts in the growth of Newport. Following the principles established by Roger Williams with the founding of the Rhode Island Colony, freedom of conscience prevailed in the minds and civic affairs of the Newport settlers, while the shape of land and sea determined the physical form of their town. Acreage was divided among farms throughout the rolling hills and broad meadowlands of the southern portion of Aquidneck Island and early dwellings appeared around a natural spring at the juncture of present-day Touro and Spring Streets. The significance of the spring in the early years of settlement is evident in its role as the starting point for measuring the distance to One Mile Corner at the northern border of Newport. It was also the point for measuring the southern border at Miles End, the present-day juncture of Thames and Pope Streets. Streams emanating from the spring also determined the course of winding streets following the direction of these freshwater sources toward Broad Street, now known as Broadway, to the northeast, and Marlborough Street, to the west, where the Great Common was established nearby along two rivulets.[7] Order was soon imposed on this relatively informal pattern of early urban development. In March 1639, the General Assembly ordered Nicholas Easton, John Clarke, and William Dyer to formally lay out streets, "Determined & Understood That They are to Run Upon Straight lines from Mark to mark, & so the good land to be Regulated accordingly & Others Also whom it may Concern."[8] A year later, in March 1640, the General Assembly followed up on its initial orders and with detailed instructions:

> *according to order, Mr. Nicholas Easton, Mr. John Clarke, and Mr. W. Dyer are appointed to lay out the streets and lands as by the Judge and Elders were proportioned forth … that all Sea Banks are free for Fishing to the Towne of Newport … that such as shall bring in their*

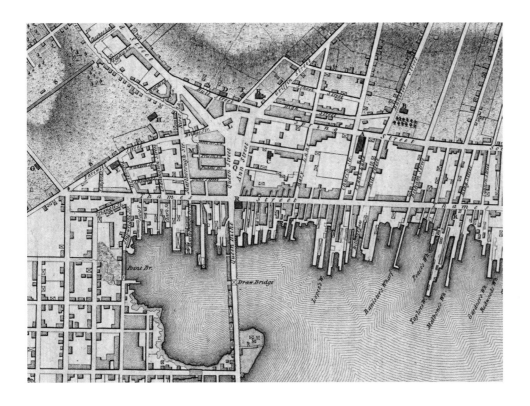

Fig. 3

Charles Blaskowitz, *Plan of the Towne of Newport* (detail), 1777. Library of Congress.

This map is the most comprehensive document of Newport's urban plan up to the late eighteenth century. The V-shaped Parade, Long Wharf, Thames Street, Spring Street, Broad Street, and the district known as the Point are clearly delineated and all major buildings are listed. Wharves and architectural landmarks are given primacy of place in the plan, evidence of the significance of commerce and the grand buildings funded in large part by the wealth produced by maritime trade.

aquittances from the Treasurer to the Judge and Elders, shall have their land recorded.[9]

The full force of the law determined the methodical disposition and documentation of land as the town plan began to take shape, with particular attention given to waterfront access. Thames Street, running on a straight north–south axis, became the spine of the city and the entry point for wharves on the harbor. Spring Street, running parallel to Thames, formed the eastern boundary of the town. These two main thoroughfares established the basic form of the colonial quarter, bordered on the north by the spring and the area that would come to be known as the "Parade," later renamed Washington Square (Fig. 3). To the south, the streets terminated at marshland at the end of the harbor. Set in a low-lying area between two hills and leading to open countryside,

Broad Street extended in a northeasterly direction from the zone between the spring and the waterfront. The completion of this early network of streets is confirmed by a 1654 letter by William Dyer, who wrote of "High Wayes Lay'd out by Mr. Nicholas Easton, Mr. John Clarke and myself" which extended from the spring to the seaside and southward.[10]

Farming and fishing provided sustenance for the first decades of settlement until the inhabitants turned to sea trade. Narrow lots ran from the hillside on the east down to the wharves on the west-facing waterfront. This model of land organization was typical in New England coastal communities from Portsmouth, New Hampshire; and Boston, Salem, and Marblehead, Massachusetts; to Stonington and Saybrook, Connecticut. In these communities, the sea banks were assessed at a high value and wharves were major financial investments and engines of economic growth.

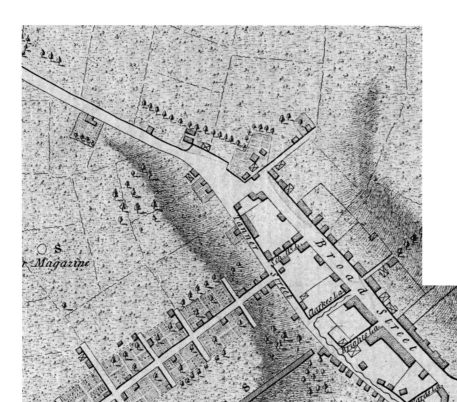

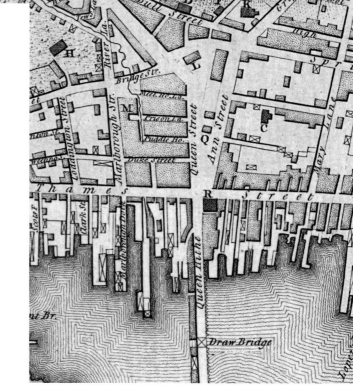

Figs. 4 and 5

Charles Blaskowitz, *Plan of the Towne of Newport* (detail), 1777. Library of Congress.

Detail of Tanner Street *(left)*, indicating the streams which determine the location of the thoroughfare and the siting of tanneries and other businesses requiring a water source.

The map *(below)* depicts the core of the original street plan set down by the founders of Newport in 1639, with an emphasis on the main thoroughfares of Thames Street, Spring Street, and Broad Street and the triangular area known as the Parade.

The significance of commerce in Newport became apparent in the 1680s when several merchants organized the Proprietors of Long Wharf to construct a wharf extending far into the harbor from the bottom of present-day Washington Square across the cove to Easton's Point.[11] This allowed for the accommodation of larger ships and the subsequent expansion of sea trade. Among a multitude of docking facilities, Long Wharf became the primary point of entry and departure from Newport and a major presence on the harbor. Tanneries rose along the waterway adjacent to Tanner Street (Figs. 4 and 5), now Dr. Marcus Wheatland Boulevard, while sawmills, breweries, ropewalks, and other shops supporting shipbuilding and maritime activities lined the burgeoning streets of a community numbering over four hundred houses by the late seventeenth century.[12]

Residential and commercial buildings increased in number, but there were very few religious structures. *A Short Account of the Present State of New England* (1690) stated, "here is a medley of most Perswasians butt neither church nor meeting house, except for one built for the use of Quakers, who are very numerous."[13] No single house of worship served as a focal point, as in the nearby Puritan Massachusetts Bay Colony (Fig. 6). Freedom to pursue personal beliefs and business preoccupied the residents as Newport grew into one of the major seaports of British North America. Wharves, houses, and shops defined the streetscapes of the entrepreneurial colonial city. However, it lacked grandeur. With the mercantile wealth of the ensuing century, Newport's plan and skyline would be distinguished by notable landmarks.

Fig. 6

John Perry Newell, *Newport in 1730*, 1844, lithograph. Newport Historical Society, 01.953.

Based on an eighteenth-century overmantel painting of Newport, this lithograph celebrates the city's position as a prominent colonial seaport. The cityscape is purposely depicted from the perspective of the harbor, with an emphasis on ships, wharves, and the steeples of houses of worship built by various religious sects—evidence of a community where freedom of conscience produced a cosmopolitan society. Of note, Newell dated the image 1730, but the Colony House, built from 1739 to 1741, appears in the skyline in the upper left as indicated by its octagonal cupola. Thus, this skyline actually reflects Newport in the 1740s. Fort George, on Goat Island, is in the foreground.

Case Study #1

Native Americans on the Land in Rhode Island and the Arrival of the English

DAVID J. SILVERMAN, PhD

PROFESSOR OF HISTORY, THE GEORGE WASHINGTON UNIVERSITY

THE ENGLISH WHO FOUNDED THE TOWNS OF Newport and Portsmouth on Aquidneck Island in the late 1630s did not enter a new world or wilderness. Indigenous people had inhabited southern New England for at least twelve thousand years, during which they had experienced numerous waves of change. Some major historical developments were still in process when the English arrived on the scene. Rather than English colonization representing a sharp break with the indigenous past, we should instead understand the colonists of Aquidneck Island and Rhode Island Colony in general as becoming part of a Native American world of intertribal politics and trade. It would take decades for colonists to seize control of the region.

People first appear in the archaeological record of southern New England about twelve thousand years ago as small bands of hunter-gatherers tracking big game like mammoths, caribou, mastodons, and giant beavers. It was a much colder time in which so much water was trapped in ice that the sea level was ten meters below its present mark, making it possible to walk across most parts of Narragansett Bay that now lie underwater, including the channel between Portsmouth and Little Compton. Then, over the next several thousand years, the warming of the earth and the melting of the last great glaciers forced a retreat of the tundra and the creation of the deciduous forests we now associate with southern New England. The big game animals disappeared with the ice, and people refocused the chase on smaller species of the emerging woodlands, such as deer, moose, bears, rabbits, and foxes. To improve their yield, people occasionally made controlled burns of the forest, which cleared out the underbrush that impeded the hunters' pursuit and created environments in which deer, beavers, hares, porcupines, and turkeys thrived.

Glacial retreat followed by rising seas formed Rhode Island's well-watered landscape of bays, inlets, rivers, ponds, and marshes and supported a bevy of wild foods to sustain human populations. There was a stunning variety of salt- and freshwater fish, waterfowl, and, of course, shellfish. The Gardiner Pond Shell Midden (or ancient trash heap) in Middletown, dated to around 80–220 CE, provides ample archaeological evidence of this sort of bounty in the form of an untold number of discarded shells. Between the estuaries and the wood line grew wild fruits like beach plums, raspberries, strawberries, and grapes. Herds of harbor seals lay basking in the sun on coastal rocks and remote beaches. To take advantage of such resources, people crafted dugout canoes (or *mishoons*) sometimes capable of carrying dozens of men and navigating miles out to sea.

The growing availability of food along the coast encouraged people to remain in specific territories year-round. Beginning in the Early Archaic period (8000–6000 BCE), they began following a seasonal round in which they spent the spring at riverside fish runs, summer along the shoreline, and fall and winter inland to hunt terrestrial animals. By and large, Native people still adhered to this pattern when colonists first arrived. By at least the Late Archaic period (3000–1000 BCE), there were several seasonal habitations on Aquidneck Island, evident in the archaeological sites preserved underneath Newport's Great Friends Meeting House. Other archaeological sites on nearby Conanicut Island show evidence of human occupation from 2500 BCE, such as the remains of house frames, hearths, trash pits, and

tools. Conanicut also has an ancient cemetery with remains dating back to 1280 BCE. Clearly Native people had a sense of proprietorship to the places in which they lived.

If the growing territoriality of indigenous people represented a major change, more revolutionary still was the arrival of the bow and arrow and of maize and bean cultivation around 700 CE (known as the Middle Woodland period). The bow and arrow, which had been adopted thousands of years earlier by Arctic peoples, was a vast improvement over the spear in terms of range and portability. It instantly improved the efficiency of hunting and probably also became a weapon of war. Maize and beans came from a different direction. These crops arose in Mexico some six thousand years ago, then spread through what is now the southwestern United States and up the Mississippi and Ohio Rivers before arriving in the Northeast. The expansion of maize was a stunning feat of human engineering in which cultivators—certainly women, given their responsibility for the crop—bred ever-larger cobs and elected seeds that could grow in colder, wetter environments.

Southern New England was the last place in America to which maize spread. The crop cannot be cultivated successfully any farther north than lower Maine. Adding horticultural produce to wild foods enabled indigenous people in southern New England, particularly along Narragansett Bay, to sustain populations as dense as those found anywhere in Native America. The overall population for southern New England circa 1600 CE was between 126,000 and 144,000 people, with the Wampanoags on the east side of Narragansett Bay boasting between 21,000 and 24,000 people and the Narragansetts on the west side some 30,000 people. It would take colonists in southern New England over a century before their numbers reached the collective heights of these groups.

When the English began settling in Narragansett Bay in the mid- to late 1630s, the political relations of indigenous people along Narragansett Bay were in flux. The primary Wampanoag sachem Ousamequin (or Massasoit) lived in the village of Sowams at the head of the Mount Hope peninsula, where the Taunton River empties into the east side of Narragansett Bay, a stone's throw north of what became the town of Portsmouth. Yet not long before, Ousamequin's people had occupied the head of Narragansett Bay, where the city of Providence is now located, as well as Aquidneck, and battled with the Narragansetts for territory and tributaries on the west bank. By the time the English arrived on the scene, the Narragansetts had driven the Wampanoags east of the Providence and Seekonk Rivers.

Neither the Wampanoags nor the Narragansetts left any statement on record of what their rivalry was about, but there are several possible explanations. One is that the Wampanoags fought for control of the planting grounds of Narragansett Bay, which were among the richest in the region. The explorer Giovanni da Verrazzano visited the bay in 1524, becoming the first European to record a venture to southern New England. As recorded in remarks published in *The Voyages of Giovanni da Verrazzano, 1524–1528*, edited by Lawrence C. Wroth, he noted that its "fields extend for 25 to 30 leagues; they are open and free of any obstacles or trees, and so fertile that any kind of seed would produce excellent crops." Some of the earliest archaeological evidence for horticulture among southern New England Indians comes from Narragansett Bay. Given how quickly maize exhausts the soil, it seems likely that the tens of thousands of Narragansetts and Wampanoags living along this estuary would have competed for the best tracts.

Another possible point of tension between the Wampanoags and Narragansetts was that they were both under pressure from the fearsome Mohawks, located just west of the modern city of Albany, New York, to produce shell beads for them. Given that the Mohawks began acquiring disc-shaped beads of quahog and periwinkle from southern New England at least as early as the sixteenth century, and that Narragansetts of the seventeenth century were known to send shell beads to the Mohawks regularly, it stands to reason that the Narragansetts and Wampanoags would compete for tributaries and try to reduce each other to tributary status in order to acquire the shells and labor to produce those beads in large quantities. At play in this contest were the shellfish-rich communities of Coweset, Shawomet, and Pawtuxet on the northwest side of Narragansett Bay, with the Narragansett tribe ultimately proving triumphant.

A final consideration is that the Wampanoags and Narragansetts fought for control of Narragansett Bay in order to control access to European trade vessels, which began to appear intermittently at least as early as 1524 and regularly by at least the early 1600s. Native people clamored after the Europeans' metal tools and implements, brightly colored cloth, mirrors, glass beads, and other jewelry. They especially prized European copper goods that resembled high-status indigenous productions of surface-mined copper acquired through long-distance, intertribal networks. For sachems of a densely populated horticultural region trying to consolidate and extend their followings against competitors, securing a new source of exotic, luxury goods with which they could reward their supporters was a potential boon.

Whatever the source of the Wampanoag-Narragansett dispute, the advantage went to the Narragansetts after an unidentified European epidemic disease devastated the Wampanoags from 1616 to 1619, more than halving their population and wiping out some villages entirely. The Narragansetts escaped the disaster, apparently because of their limited contact with infected Wampanoags. The Narragansetts used this newfound advantage to force the Wampanoags from the head of Narragansett Bay and the islands, including Aquidneck.

The Wampanoag-Narragansett rivalry was the backdrop to the first decades of English colonization on Narragansett Bay. When Roger Williams fled Massachusetts in the winter of 1636, he first sought refuge with Ousamequin, who placed him at a site east of the Seekonk River at the head of the bay. Williams had been cultivating this relationship for years as a fur trader. When the Plymouth colony warned Williams out of this area, he relocated

just a few miles west to an area at the confluence of the Moshassuck and Woonasquatucket Rivers, the intermediate zone between the Wampanoags and Narragansetts. He called the place Providence. Both Ousamequin and the Narragansett sachem Canonicus supported this move for similar reasons. For one, an English settlement would serve as a buffer against the other's raids. It would also provide them with readier access to English goods and services, including the use of Williams as a go-between and scribe in their relations with other tribes and colonies. As Williams told, the Wampanoags and Narragansetts used him as "their counselor and secretary … they had my person, my shallop and pinnace, and hired servant, etc., at command, on all occasions, transporting 50 at a time." In other words, Williams, by virtue of living in their country, had become their resource.

Over the next decade, Ousamequin granted Williams and other Rhode Island colonists the right to settle and use tracts all around the northern and eastern edges of Narragansett Bay and its islands, including Aquidneck, within the Wampanoag-Narragansett no-man's-land. The Narragansetts did the same, ceding land north of their core territory which the Wampanoags contested. To be sure, the English compensated the sachems for these grants—for instance, paying Ousamequin five fathoms of wampum for the right to graze livestock in what became the town of Portsmouth. However, Williams knew that these sums were merely one aspect of what the sachems expected in return. They were cultivating the English as friends to advise their people in politics, defend them in times of danger, and treat them with respect and hospitality. Williams explained, in letters recorded in *The Correspondence of Roger Williams*, edited by Glenn W. LaFantasie, that he secured the sachems' consent to build at Providence "not by monies or payment ... monies could not do it." Rather, "what was paid was only a gratuity, though I choose, for better assurance and form, to call it a sale." Such transactions were not one-for-one exchanges of land for goods, but a mutual pledge to sustain "a loving and peaceable neighborhood." Ousamequin captured this spirit in the deed for Portsmouth, stressing that he expected William Coddington and his associates to pursue a "loving and just carriage" toward the sachem, his followers, and their posterity—always (remarks recorded in the Records of the Colony of Rhode Island and Providence Plantations in New England).

It is telling of Indian power along Narragansett Bay that English Rhode Islanders generally adhered to Indian expectations about joint use of the land and satisfied Wampanoag and Narragansett complaints about violations, if out of self-preservation rather than moral principle. As Williams put it to the Massachusetts legislature in 1655, Rhode Island's "dangers (being a frontier people to the Barbarians) are greater than those of other colonies." Yet the Aquidneck English passed laws that ran contrary to the spirit of mutuality—even if they did not enforce them (as appears to have been the case)—which foreshadowed the issues that would drive Indians and colonists to war by the mid-1670s. As late as the 1660s, the total population of colonial Rhode Island

was still only about 1,500 people, or about one-tenth the size of just the Narragansetts, so the colonists were hardly in a position to dictate to Native people. Regionally, however, the English had a greater advantage, and they used it to expand their land, jurisdiction, and religion at the expense of Native peoples in colonies like Massachusetts, Plymouth, and eventually Rhode Island too.

The result was King Philip's War of 1675–76, in which the allied Wampanoags, Narragansetts, Nipmucs, and other indigenous people initially devastated English towns throughout Plymouth, Rhode Island, and Massachusetts, only to be defeated within a year at the hands of the colonies and their coalition of Indian allies. It took that war for the English to seize control of the region, including Aquidneck, by killing and enslaving thousands of Native people and seizing their territory. Even then, there remained small communities of Narragansett and Wampanoag survivors, who still considered Aquidneck a Native place with a deep Native history. Their descendants retain that sense of connection to this very day.

Opposite

John Speed, A Map of New England and New York, 1676. Newport Historical Society, 2009.6.

This map depicts New England as a land ripe for exploration—all gunkholes, wild animals, and Indian nations, including names both real and imagined. Not created for New World residents but primarily for seventeenth-century armchair travelers abroad, the map transmits the excitement of the idea of discovery.

A Map of NEW ENGLAND AND NEW YORK
Sold by Tho. Basset in Fleetstreet, and Richard Chiswell in St Pauls Church yard.

EVOLUTIONS

Civic Splendor in the Eighteenth Century

"The town had grown to the admiration of all."

Newport Town Council, 1712

DURING THE EARLY 1700S, NEWPORT'S RISE
as a seaport with increasing wealth and population
coincided with the commission for a survey of streets
from John Mumford (Fig. 7).[14] Unlike the few formally
planned cities in British North America, such as New
Haven, Connecticut (1638), Annapolis, Maryland
(1695), and Savannah, Georgia (1733), which from
inception featured regular grids of streets and broad
avenues focused on buildings and public squares,
Newport followed a more typical colonial format of
organic growth providing no specified lots of land
for the presentation of impressive architecture.[15]
Churches, meetinghouses, and civic structures had
to take their places in an already established system
of streets among the domiciles, workshops, and
warehouses of merchants, artisans, and laborers.

The Great Friends Meeting House (1699) was
the first large-scale building to appear in Newport.
Facing the Great Common, its shingled facades and
lack of ornament expressed the Quaker aesthetic of

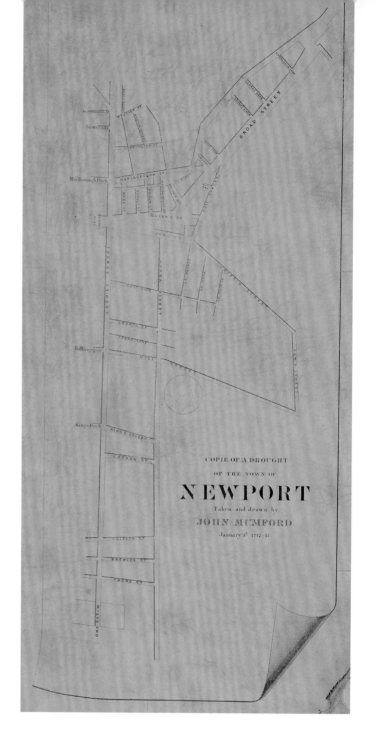

Fig. 7

Map of the Township of Newport and Middletown
(detail), from Sarony, Major and Knapp Lithographers,
Coastal Survey Department, ca. 1860. Courtesy of
Mr. & Mrs. S. Matthews V. Hamilton, Jr.

The detail depicts John Mumford's 1712 map of
Newport's streets.

plainness (Fig. 8). Trinity Church (1726) was designed by Richard Munday, who gave the Newport cityscape a house of worship with a galleried two-story hall and spire inspired by the London churches of Sir Christopher Wren. The Society for the Propagation of the Gospel in Foreign Parts, a Church of England missionary organization, produced pattern books to encourage architectural uniformity for Anglican churches across the burgeoning British Empire.[16] Munday's work adhered to its English prototypes. Set on a narrow plot bordered by Spring, Church, and Frank Streets, Trinity Church had little decoration

Fig. 8

The Great Friends Meeting House, ca. 1840, print. Newport Historical Society, 2004.13.216.

The Great Friends Meeting House is presented in this print as a major landmark infused with the romantic spirit of the Colonial Revival.

Fig. 9

John Perry Newell, *Newport in 1730* (detail), 1844, lithograph. Newport Historical Society, 01.953.

on its lower floors since neighboring houses clustered around its base (Fig. 9). No public square or green provided a vantage point for the building. The spire, however, became a constant landmark offering a complex arrangement of classical arches, obelisks, and urns to mark the skyline.

Richard Munday introduced a baroque richness to the urban landscape of Newport. After the successful completion of Trinity Church, he undertook work on the Colony House (1739–41). Placed between the town spring and the triangular-shaped area of open land referred to as the "Parade," the

Colony House (Figs. 10–12) functioned as the architectural anchor of an expansive civic space. Its main elevation faced west toward Long Wharf. Individuals disembarking from ships were presented with a view toward the grand brick and brownstone building with a gilded pineapple atop its elaborately carved central pediment. Thus, the first sweeping urban vista in Newport did not include a religious building, but a government house approached from a commercial wharf. Created after the establishment of its surrounding streets, Munday's building took advantage of its physical situation to maximum effect. On the north and south sides of the Parade rose the houses of prominent merchants (Figs. 13–19), each residence reinforcing the power of a mercantile elite within the shadow of its government and market buildings. The final ensemble of the Colony House, the Parade, and Long Wharf heralded a new scale of civic splendor, a reflection of the economic factors of booming sea trade and the taste

for architectural landmarks that characterized the eighteenth-century city.

While the Colony House marked the center of Newport, a building of a distinctly different character rose to the east in the meadowlands above the city. The Redwood Library began with a circle of intellectually minded merchants, ministers, and scholars and a plot of land on the outskirts of the town. In 1729, a group of residents formed the Philosophical Society for "the propagation of knowledge and virtue through a free conversation."[17] The members combined their collections of books,

Fig. 10

View of the Colony House, ca. 1885, photograph. Newport Historical Society, P5369.

The Colony House, a visual landmark in the center of the city, was the focal point of the Parade which led to Long Wharf. Richly carved wooden pilasters and a broken pediment housing a pineapple frame the main door, window, and balcony of the building. Built of red brick, with brownstone imported from Connecticut for the window and door trims, the Colony House stood out in a city of wooden structures. This photograph depicts the building in its nineteenth-century guise.

Fig. 11

Detail of the Colony House, ca. 1947, photograph. Newport Historical Society, Robert Meservey Collection, P9402.

Richard Munday's design is marked by the boldness of its carved wooden cornices and the cupola which dominates the skyline. Inspired by the great houses and public buildings of late seventeenth- and early eighteenth-century England, Munday created one of the most richly decorated public structures in Newport, reflecting the increasing economic and cultural prestige of the city.

Fig. 12

Colony House, ca. 1885, photograph. Newport Historical Society, P9401.

Fig. 13

Unidentified artist, Detail of Washington Square,
1818, painting. Newport Historical Society, 94.4.1.

Fig. 14

View of Washington Square, ca. 1880, photograph. Newport Historical Society, P2371.

The Mumford House (far right) and the Odd Fellows Hall (far left) represent the two faces of Washington Square: the old and the new. The Mumford House displays the domestic scale and classical forms of the eighteenth century; the Odd Fellows Hall, with its large plate glass windows and Italianate details, is a product of the industrial technology and tastes of the Victorian age.

Fig. 15

View of Charles Street, ca. 1880, photograph. Newport Historical Society, P4314.

Charles Street maintained its eighteenth-century buildings intact until the demolition, or removal, of houses on the left side of the street in the mid-twentieth century.

Fig. 16 *(right)*

Detail of the eighteenth-century Mumford House on Washington Square, ca. 1890, photograph. Newport Historical Society, P2373.

Fig. 17 *(below)*

View of the Stephen Decatur House, ca. 1890, photograph. Newport Historical Society, P9483.

The Decatur House (ca. 1714), owned in the mid-eighteenth century by the French mariner Etienne Decatur, whose grandson, Stephen Decatur III, became a renowned naval commander. Originally located on the site of the present courthouse in Washington Square, the Decatur House was moved to Charles Street in the early 1830s.

Fig. 18

Marlborough Street, 1920, photograph. Newport
Historical Society, P66.

First laid out in the seventeenth century along a
freshwater rivulet flowing westward toward the
harbor, Marlborough Street has undergone significant
change since its inception. This photograph
documents the intact eighteenth- and nineteenth-
century buildings defining the streetscape before mid-
twentieth-century demolition for parking lots.

Fig. 19

Marlborough Street, 1952, photograph.
Newport Historical Society, P73.

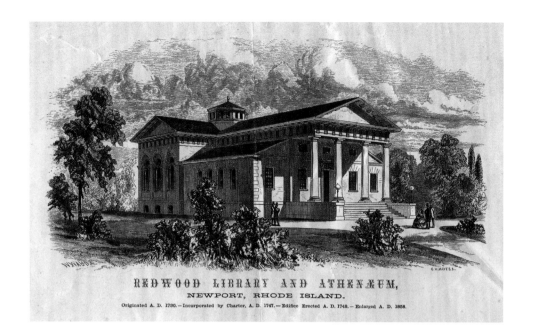

REDWOOD LIBRARY AND ATHENÆUM,
NEWPORT, RHODE ISLAND.
Originated A. D. 1730. — Incorporated by Charter, A. D. 1747. — Edifice Erected A. D. 1748. — Enlarged A. D. 1858.

Fig. 20 *(left)*

G. H. Hayes, *Redwood Library and Athenaeum*, 1859, print. Newport Historical Society, 2004.13.56.

Fig. 21 *(opposite)*

Ezra Stiles, Map of the City and Harbor of Newport, 1758 (detail). Redwood Library and Athenaeum, RLA B65N.

As the librarian of the Redwood Library, a founder of Brown University, and a president of Yale University, Ezra Stiles was a major intellectual presence in eighteenth-century Newport. His map is one of the earliest documents of the city plan.

which soon required a proper place for use and storage. In 1747, the Philosophical Society, renamed the Company of the Redwood Library, engaged Peter Harrison to devise a building worthy of their classical tastes. Aided by his own superlative library of architectural pattern books, Harrison created one of the earliest Neo-Palladian temple forms in British North America. Such a noble edifice would usually be the focal point of an avenue, square, or prominent hill. Not so in Newport. A gift by Henry Collins determined the location of this monument to learning. One of Newport's richest merchants and patrons, Collins donated his bowling green on a hillcrest above town for the purpose of building the library. Thus, the structure stood in isolation among fields, the result of a practical gift rather than purposeful placement. Although not initially perceived as Newport's version of an ancient temple on an acropolis, the effect, however, was still august. A Roman portico rising on the green fields of Newport proclaimed both the cultural aspirations and architectural sophistication of the age (Fig. 20). Harrison established his career and went on to endow Newport's streetscapes with some of the finest public buildings of the colonial era, the Brick Market (1762) and Touro Synagogue (1763).

Interest in Newport's evolving cityscape is evident in a map drawn in 1758 by the Reverend Ezra Stiles (Fig. 21). This eminent theologian and scholar served as the minister of the Second Congregational Church, librarian of Redwood Library, a founder of Brown University, and, later, president of Yale University. He did not approach the making of his map as a skilled cartographer, but as a man of the Enlightenment, as one dedicated to documenting the empirical data of his environment. Religious structures and the Colony House are clearly listed along with various types of shops and houses (Fig. 22). The balance between public structures and the economic engines of the wharves is clearly delineated. The Parade appears as a triangle dominated to the west by Long Wharf and to the east by the Colony House. To the south,

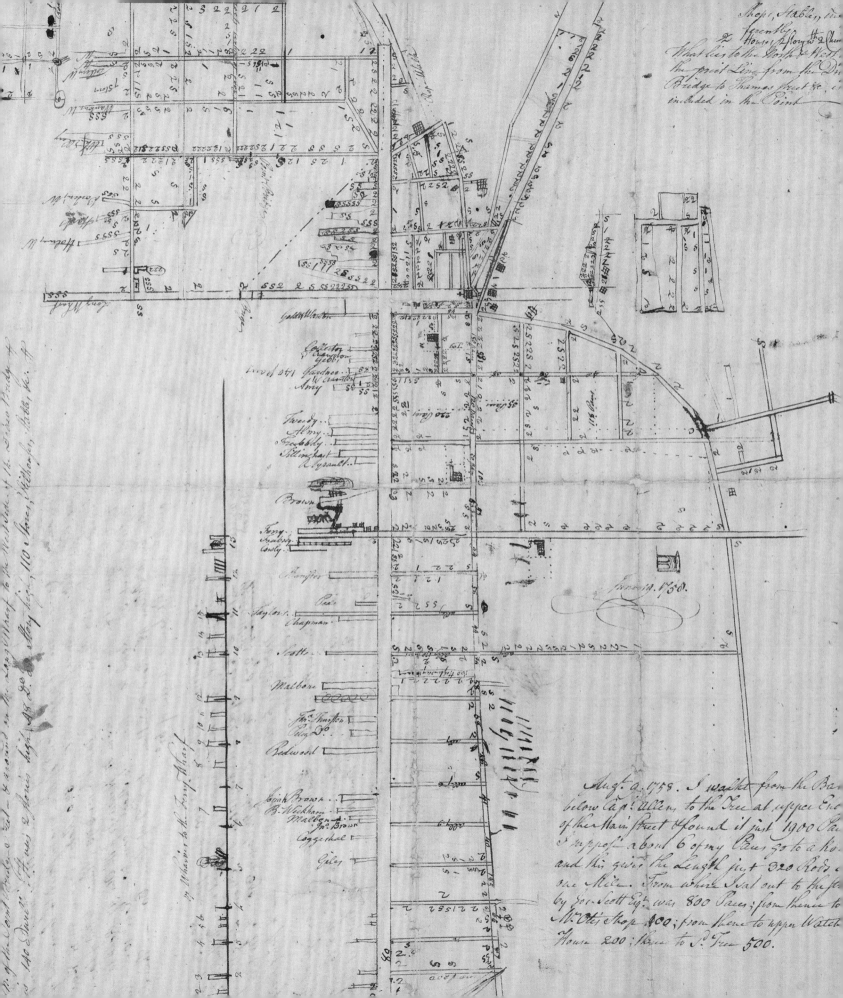

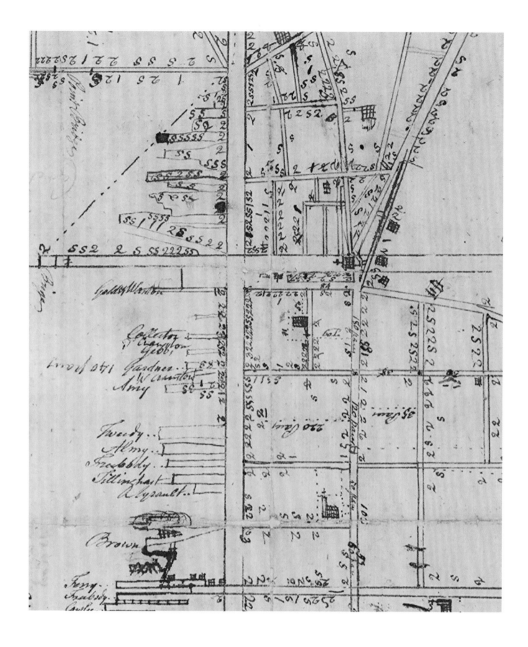

Fig. 22 (*left*)

Ezra Stiles, Map of the City and Harbor of Newport (detail), 1758. Redwood Library and Athenaeum, RLA B65N.

Stiles marked houses by number: 1 indicates a one-story building; 2 designates a two-story building.

Fig. 23 (*opposite*)

Detail of Washington Square in the mid-1850s, from Matthew Dripps and B.I. Tilley, *Map of the City of Newport* (New York and Newport, RI, 1859). Newport Historical Society.

Washington Square maintained its original eighteenth-century form in plan, yet it continually evolved in terms of the addition of new types of buildings and the infill of open lots.

Stiles recorded Thames and Spring Streets and the long, narrow blocks created by the cross streets leading directly to the wharves. To the northwest of the Parade is the planned grid of the Point and in a northeasterly direction is Broad Street, including listings of its numerous residences and commercial buildings.

Although not initially envisioned as the focal point of Newport, the Parade evolved into the city's visual heart. Long Wharf and the location of the central triangular grass plot defined the general shape of the area (Figs. 23–29). The placement of the Colony House at the head of this open zone in 1741 established a formal axis.

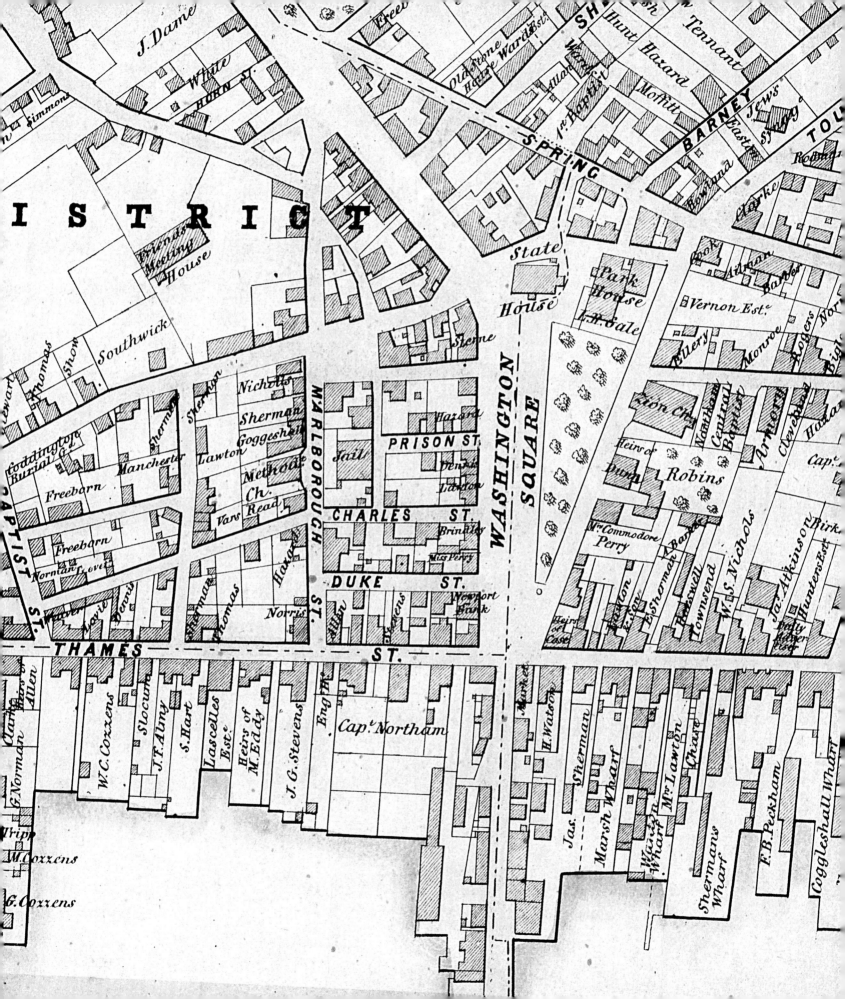

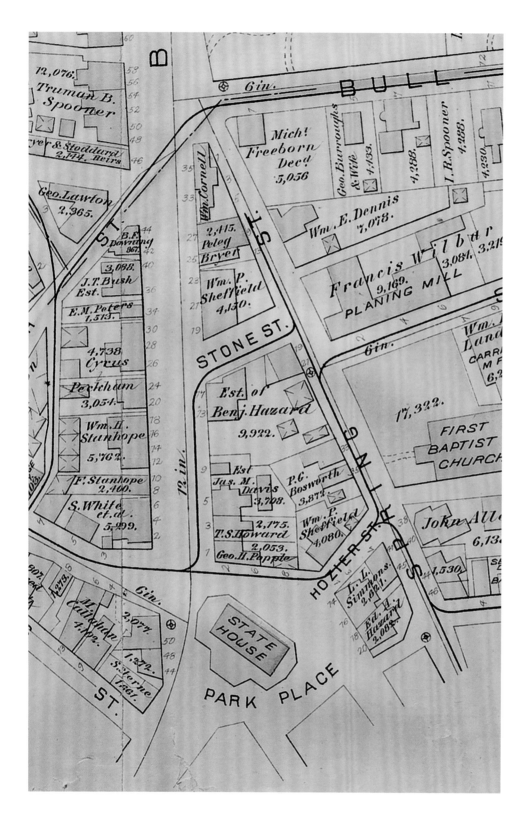

Fig. 24 *(left)*

Washington Square, from G. M. Hopkins, *City Atlas of Newport, Rhode Island* (Philadelphia, 1883). Newport Historical Society. Photograph courtesy of the Preservation Society of Newport County.

Fig. 25 *(opposite)*

Washington Square, from L. J. Richards and Co., *Atlas of the City of Newport* (Springfield, MA, 1893). Newport Historical Society. Photography courtesy of the Preservation Society of Newport County.

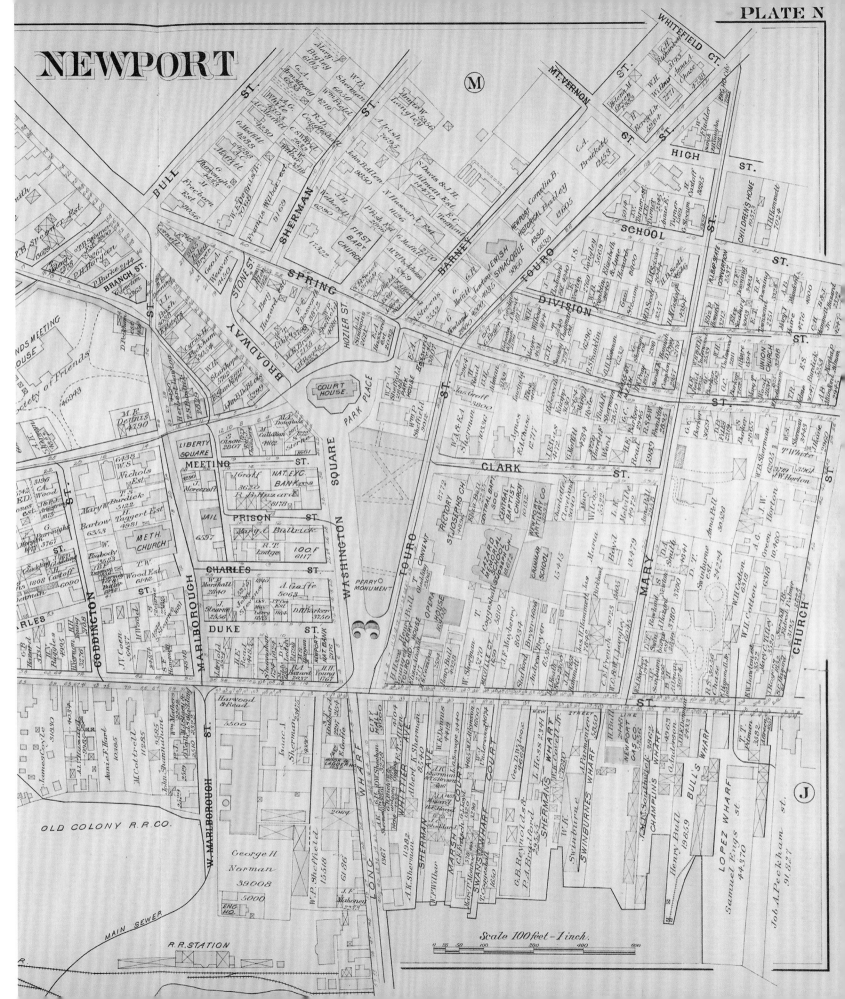

Fig. 26

The Old Quarter, from *Atlas of Newport, Jamestown, Middletown and Portsmouth, RI* (New York: Sanborn Map and Publishing, 1921). Newport Historical Society. Photograph courtesy of the Preservation Society of Newport County.

Washington Square, Thames Street, and the Historic Hill in 1921. Streetcars, indicated by a broken black line, traverse the square toward Long Wharf. Electric railway streetcars were introduced to Newport in 1889.

Fig. 27

Colony House at the eastern end of Washington Square, ca. 1885, photograph. Newport Historical Society, P8620.

Fig. 28

Park House (left) and the Levi Gale House (right) at the eastern end of Washington Square, ca. 1915, photograph. Newport Historical Society, P2383.

The Park House was demolished and the Levi Gale House moved by the early 1900s for the construction of the Newport County Court House (1926).

Fig. 29

View from the Colony House to the west toward Long Wharf, ca. 1885, daguerreotype. Newport Historical Society, P9223.

Fig. 30

Unidentified artist, Detail of the Brick Market,
1818, painting. Newport Historical Society, 94.4.1.

In 1762, Peter Harrison enhanced the Square
with his design for the Brick Market (Fig. 30).
Entrepreneurial rather than aesthetic concerns
dictated the placement of the building. Within
easy reach of Long Wharf and the entire Thames
Street commercial zone, it was perfectly situated
as an economic center. Harrison designed a
sophisticated version of a Palladian town palace
with an arcaded first level supporting upper floors
marked by monumental two-story half columns
in the Ionic style (Figs. 31–33). Andrea Palladio's

urban work in sixteenth-century Italy provided the
models, particularly his buildings in Vicenza, which
assertively addressed the need for utility and the
desire for beauty. Arcades and open colonnades
opening onto streets and squares were dominant
features of his designs for houses and civic buildings,
which he published in *Il Quattro Libri* (1570).
English architects discovered his work during the
early 1600s. Among the most prominent of them
was Inigo Jones, who translated Palladian forms
and features into his work for the royal family and

Fig. 31 *(far left)*

William James Stillman, Brick Market, 1875, photograph. McKim Portfolio, Newport Historical Society, P380.

The Brick Market was photographed as part of a study of eighteenth-century Newport architecture, streetscapes, furniture, and objects of historic interest commissioned by the architect Charles Follen McKim.

Fig. 32 *(left)*

Detail of arcades and Ionic pilasters on the Brick Market, ca. 1940, photograph. Newport Historical Society, P1203.

The architectural details of Peter Harrison's 1762 landmark survived through the centuries.

Fig. 33 *(below)*

Washington Square, ca. 1885, photograph. Newport Historical Society, P8615.

those aspiring to the latest architectural fashions. The arcaded façade of Somerset House, overlooking the River Thames, was one of the earliest Palladian-style city residences. Jones's terraced houses for Covent Garden (1630)—with their red brick arcaded first floors and upper floors adorned with classical pilasters—are one of the first architecturally harmonious Renaissance-inspired urban ensembles in London.[18] This building type would make its way across the Atlantic to the British colonies; in Newport, the Brick Market is one of the most sophisticated renditions of this form in British North America (Figs. 34–39).

With the Colony House and the Brick Market at its eastern and western ends, and merchant's houses lining its streets, the Parade presented itself as a stately city center (Fig. 40). Steeples of the various houses of

Fig. 34 (*above*)

Long Wharf, ca. 1880, photograph. Newport Historical Society, P1319.

Fig. 35 (*right*)

Long Wharf and Brick Market, ca. 1895, photograph. Newport Historical Society, P118.

Fig. 36 *(left)*

Signage on the Brick Market,
ca. 1920, photograph. Newport
Historical Society, P1195.

Brick Market served many functions,
from colonial trading hub to later
nineteenth-century town hall, and,
eventually, the center of several shops.

Fig. 37 *(below)*

View of Washington Square and the
Brick Market, ca. 1910, photograph.
Newport Historical Society, P2554.

Fig. 38 *(above)*

The Brick Market, ca. 1940, photograph. Newport Historical Society, P1203.

Fig. 39 *(right)*

Washington Square and Brick Market in the 1938 hurricane, 1938, photograph. Newport Historical Society, 2019.017.012.

The Brick Market has been a constant landmark in an ever-changing cityscape. It has survived war, a variety of uses, hurricanes, and nearby demolitions for urban renewal.

Fig. 40

Unidentified artist, Detail of Washington Square, 1818, painting. Newport Historical Society, 94.4.1.

The artist depicts the architectural elegance of Washington Square in this view of grand Georgian houses and the fashionably dressed on promenade.

worship may have begun to mark Newport's general skyline, but a government building and a market house dominated its main square. Providence, founded in 1636 at the northern terminus of Narragansett Bay, had a development similar to Newport. Founded by Roger Williams, who established the principle of freedom of conscience in the colony of Rhode Island, Providence consisted of narrow plots of land extending from the waterfront to farmlands. By the late eighteenth century, the Market House (1775) and the First Baptist Church (1775) were Providence's primary landmarks. They were situated, much like Newport's grand buildings, not as the focal point of grand squares or avenues but inserted into an existing streetscape. Politics and commerce, rather than religion, ruled in colonial Rhode Island communities and is clearly evident in Newport's urban scenery. Thus, the heart of Newport is the physical manifestation of freedom of conscience and the realities of maritime trade.

Touro Synagogue (1763) is one of the finest and final landmarks of the religious liberty and commercial wealth of Newport during the British colonial era. Peter Harrison's masterpiece for the Congregation Jeshuat Israel was a testament to the community of Sephardic Jews from Portugal who had established themselves as a thriving economic and dynamic cultural force in Newport.[19] Situated on a hill rising from the natural spring, Touro Synagogue's location afforded a prominent public profile (Fig. 41). Although it too, like all structures in Newport, had to be set not in a civic square but among domestic dwellings, it still rises high among

Fig. 41

J. A. Williams, Touro Synagogue, 1881, photograph. Newport Historical Society, P2764.

Touro Synagogue is a major feature of the Historic Hill district. Its architectural prominence is an expression in built form of the freedom of conscience that defined life in eighteenth-century Newport. Peter Harrison, who referred to his extensive architectural pattern book collection for the design, had few models to follow since most Jewish communities worshipped in private for their own safety. Harrison created a masterpiece of classical design that also served the religious practices of its congregation. Today, the building is designated a National Historic Site.

its neighbors. The religious freedoms ensured in Rhode Island's colonial charter gave impetus to the creation of a synagogue that could take its place as a true mark upon the land among other public buildings. Its unadorned exterior in the form of a simple cube belies the innovative interior arrangement, a two-galleried space featuring twelve classical columns representing the twelve tribes of Israel. Harrison's work is a tour de force of classical architecture adapting the needs of Jewish religious service with the forms of ancient Greece and Rome, reinterpreted on the shores of Rhode Island.

Newport's economy and the flourishing of its arts and crafts reached its apex in the mid-eighteenth

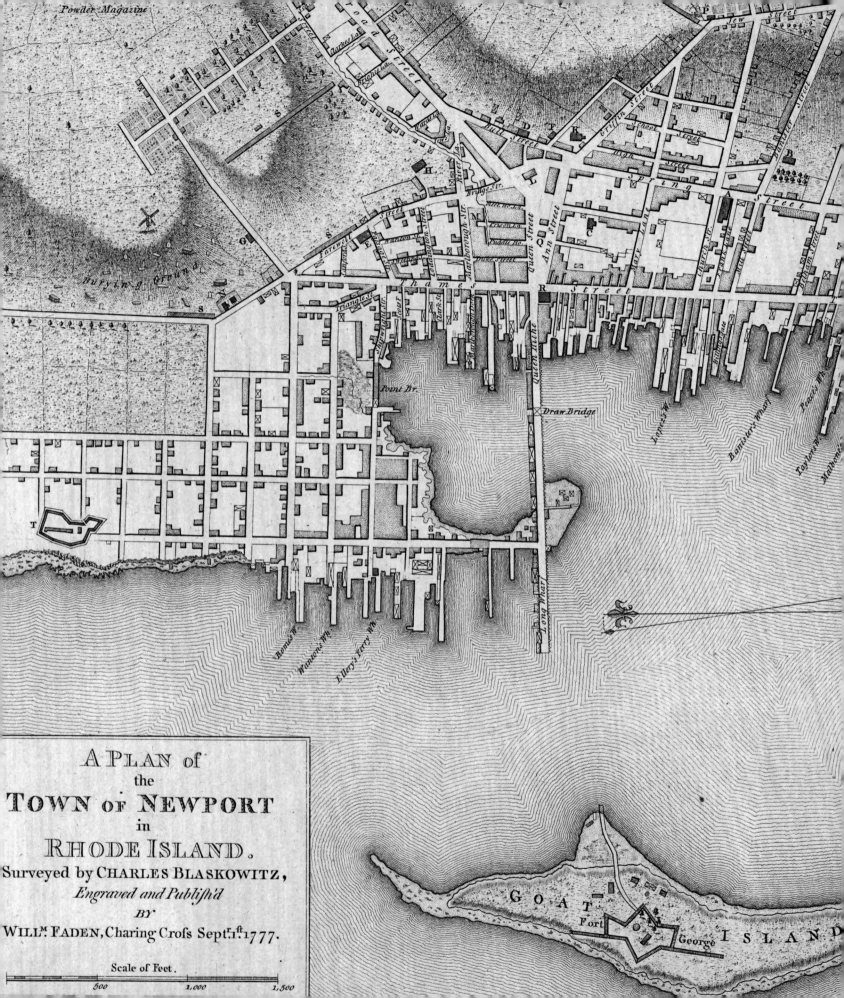

Powder Magazine

Burying Ground

Bridge Str.

Queen Wharf

Point Br.

Draw Bridge

Long Wharf

Bannister's Wharf

Peace's Wh.

Wanton's Wh.

Elbey's Ferry Wh.

Thames Street

Spring Street

A PLAN of
the
TOWN of NEWPORT
in
RHODE ISLAND.
Surveyed by CHARLES BLASKOWITZ,
Engraved and Publish'd
BY
WILLM. FADEN, Charing Cross Sept.1st 1777.

Scale of Feet.

500   1,000   1,500

GOAT ISLAND

Fort George

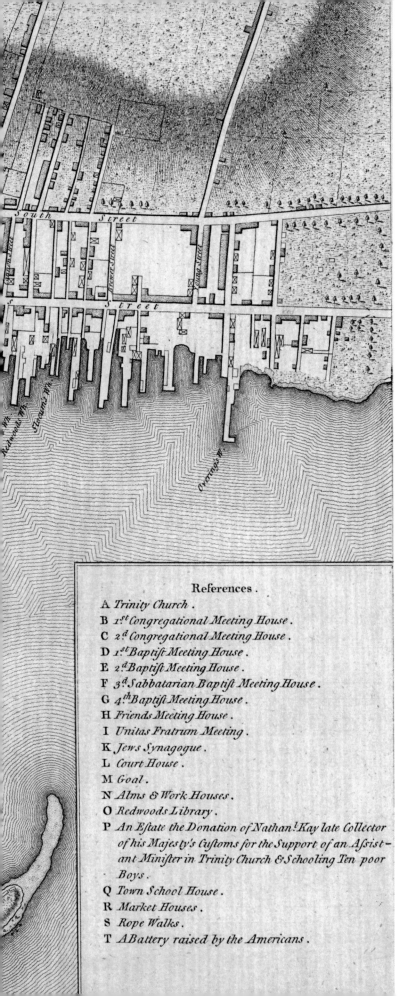

References.

A *Trinity Church*.
B *1st Congregational Meeting House*.
C *2d Congregational Meeting House*.
D *1st Baptist Meeting House*.
E *2d Baptist Meeting House*.
F *3d Sabbatarian Baptist Meeting House*.
G *4th Baptist Meeting House*.
H *Friends Meeting House*.
I *Unitas Fratrum Meeting*.
K *Jews Synagogue*.
L *Court House*.
M *Goal*.
N *Alms & Work Houses*.
O *Redwoods Library*.
P *An Estate the Donation of Nathanl Kay late Collector of his Majesty's Customs for the Support of an Assist- ant Minister in Trinity Church & Schooling Ten poor Boys*.
Q *Town School House*.
R *Market Houses*.
S *Rope Walks*.
T *A Battery raised by the Americans*.

century. Charles Blaskowitz produced a detailed plan of the city in 1777 (Fig. 42), the very year when it faced a commercial and political abyss following the declaration of independence by the American colonies. His map lists all public buildings, ropewalks, a battery, and windmills on the hills above town. Side streets extending from Spring Street to Jew Street, the present-day Bellevue Avenue, indicate the expansion of the city since Ezra Stiles's 1758 map.

Such growth, however, came to a halt with the American War of Independence. Occupation by the British from 1776 to 1779 caused social upheaval and economic downturn. No new major street layout or building would occur for the remainder of the century. After the revolution, the city ceased to be one of the leading seaports of the Eastern Seaboard, bypassed in commercial importance by Providence (to the north on Narragansett Bay) as well as Boston, Salem, New York, Philadelphia, and Baltimore. Even if the riches of the postwar era were not apparent in Newport, the spirit of the newly formed nation made its presence felt in the act of renaming streets and public spaces in the very heart of the city. The Parade and Queen Street, on its northern side, were given the new title of "Washington Square" to honor the heroic figure of George Washington and to purge the city of any royal associations.

Fig. 42

Charles Blaskowitz, *Plan of the Towne of Newport* (detail), 1777. Library of Congress.

THE OLD MEETS THE NEW

The Old Quarter in the Nineteenth and Twentieth Centuries

INDUSTRIAL REVOLUTION, HISTORICAL FANTASY, and modernist efficiency all projected themselves, in one form or another, on the colonial city during the nineteenth and twentieth centuries. On Washington Square, the once grand houses of eighteenth-century merchants were repurposed as Victorian businesses. Several Georgian buildings, their two-story facades defining the domestic scale of the streetscape, were demolished to make way for multistory Italianate-style banks and Second Empire shops (Figs. 43–54).

Fig. 43

The Merchant's and Exchange Bank on Washington Square, ca. 1885, photograph. Newport Historical Society, P2364.

Fig. 44

The Victorian era Odd Fellows Hall on the corner
of Washington Square and Charles Street, ca. 1885,
photograph. Newport Historical Society, P4835.

To the right is a colonial period house with the first
floor adapted for shops.

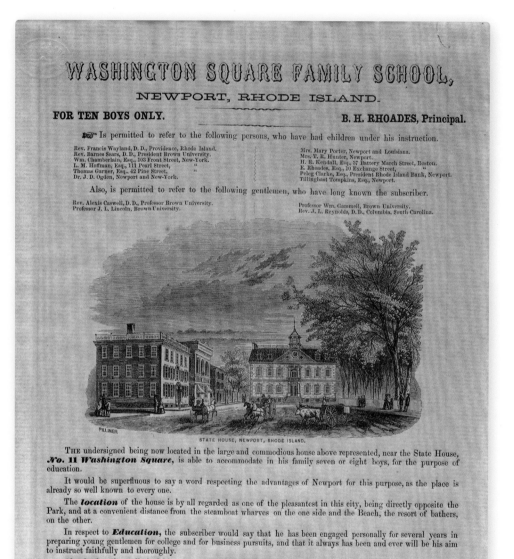

THE undersigned being now located in the large and commodious house above represented, near the State House, *No. 11 Washington Square*, is able to accommodate in his family seven or eight boys, for the purpose of education.

It would be superfluous to say a word respecting the advantages of Newport for this purpose, as the place is already so well known to every one.

The *location* of the house is by all regarded as one of the pleasantest in this city, being directly opposite the Park, and at a convenient distance from the steamboat wharves on the one side and the Beach, the resort of bathers, on the other.

In respect to *Education*, the subscriber would say that he has been engaged personally for several years in preparing young gentlemen for college and for business pursuits, and that it always has been and ever will be his aim to instruct faithfully and thoroughly.

Also, having always limited himself to a very few, he has found it a pleasure both to himself and to his pupils to accompany them in their amusements, bathing, sailing, skating, &c.

He hopes he can truthfully offer a home where there will be a careful regard for health and comfort, and where Christian principles and precepts are respected and inculcated.

Respecting terms and other arrangements, he would be happy to communicate by letter with any who may wish to place sons under his care.

Fig. 45

Handbill for the Washington Square Family School with the Colony House in the background, ca. 1857, print. Newport Historical Society, 94.4.5.

During the early nineteenth century, many residences on Washington Square were converted to various purposes. This advertisement for a school extols the benefits of its location near a steamship landing on the harbor and the nearby park in the square.

Fig. 46 *(above)*

A view to Brick Market, ca. 1915, postcard. Newport Historical Society, 2009.3.55.

Fig. 47 *(right)*

Northwest corner of Washington Square, ca. 1890, postcard. Newport Historical Society, P9886.

Fig. 48

Commercial buildings on Washington Square, ca.
1910, photograph. Newport Historical Society,
2009.3.150.

Fig. 49

Washington Square, ca. 1910, photograph. Newport Historical Society, P9365.

Fig. 50

The David Chesebrough House on Mary Street, ca. 1890, photograph. Newport Historical Society, P5712.

This house represents the evolution of many of Newport's colonial period buildings. Originally a grand private residence in the eighteenth century, it was used as a YMCA in the late nineteenth century, and was later replaced in the early twentieth century with a Georgian Revival–style YMCA (ca. 1909), built by Mrs. Cornelius Vanderbilt in memory of her husband.

Fig. 51 *(left)*

View of the northeast corner of Washington Square, ca. 1910, photograph. Newport Historical Society, P9635.

Construction work on the foundations for the Navy YMCA building is in the foreground. The Colony House is to the left and the Levi Gale House to the right. In the early 1900s, the Levi Gale House was moved to Touro Street to make way for the construction of the Newport County Court House (1926). By the 1930s, the building between the Colony House and the Levi Gale House was demolished and replaced by a gas station.

Fig. 52 *(opposite below)*

The Levi Gale House cut in half for its removal to Touro Street, ca. 1915, photograph. Newport Historical Society, P5515.

The Newport County Court House (1926) took its place on the eastern side of Washington Square.

Fig. 53 *(right)*

Construction of the Navy YMCA on Washington Square, ca. 1911, photograph. Newport Historical Society, P2371.

Fig. 54

The Perry House on Touro Street, ca. 1915, photograph. Newport Historical Society, P1822.

Home to famed naval figure Commodore Matthew C. Perry, this Georgian house from the mid-1700s had many functions and architectural modifications through the centuries, reflecting the ever-changing nature of Washington Square. First it served as a grand private house, then as a series of businesses during the nineteenth century, with plate glass windows added (as seen in this photograph). The building was restored to its colonial era appearance in the mid-twentieth century.

Fig. 55 *(left)*

Bicyclists on Washington Square, ca. 1890, photograph. Newport Historical Society, P9373.1.

Fig. 56 *(below)*

Washington Square, ca. 1900, postcard. Newport Historical Society, 2009.3.49.

The postcard depicts two modes of transportation in the early twentieth century: the horse and carriage and the electric streetcar.

In 1889, electric streetcars (Figs. 55 and 56) were introduced along Broadway, Washington Square, Spring Street, and Bath Road.[20] The square also became a place to parade and promenade, as well as the backdrop for Atlantic Fleet parties, Fourth of July celebrations, and Old Home Weeks when flags and lights decked historic buildings (Figs. 57–65).

Thames Street, the site of maritime activities since the late seventeenth century, and the Historic Hill district, composed of Spring Street and the open fields to the east, experienced increased urban infill (Figs. 66–75). The original settlement pattern composed of wharves and thin strips of land, running eastward containing houses with extensive garden plots, yielded highly valuable commercial property. Victorian hotels, warehouses, and stores filled this densely built and bustling district (Figs. 76 and 77).

WASHINGTON MALL, NEWPORT, R. I.

Fig. 57 *(right)*

"Peanut Joe" Braganzio, ca. 1915, photograph. Newport Historical Society, P9320.

Peanut Joe was a street vendor on Washington Square.

Fig. 58 *(below right)*

Parade on Washington Square, ca. 1920, photograph. Newport Historical Society, U16/P9888.

Fig. 59

Parade on Washington Square,
July 4, 1884, photograph.
Newport Historical Society, P9375.

Fig. 60

Samuel Kerschner, Atlantic Fleet
party on Washington Square,
August 16, 1922, photograph.
Newport Historical Society, P9371.

Fig. 61 *(opposite)*

Brick Market draped in flags,
May 30, 1899, photograph.
Newport Historical Society, P1205.

Fig. 62

Military parade, ca. 1900, photograph. Newport Historical Society, P1076.

Fig. 63

Atlantic Fleet party, 1915, photograph. Newport Historical Society, P8647.

Fig. 64 *(right)*

Old Home Week arch before the
Colony House, ca. 1900, photograph.
Newport Historical Society, P2362.

Fig. 65 *(below)*

Street party in front of the Navy
YMCA at the corner of Washington
Square and Broadway, ca. 1955,
photograph. Newport Historical
Society, P9369.

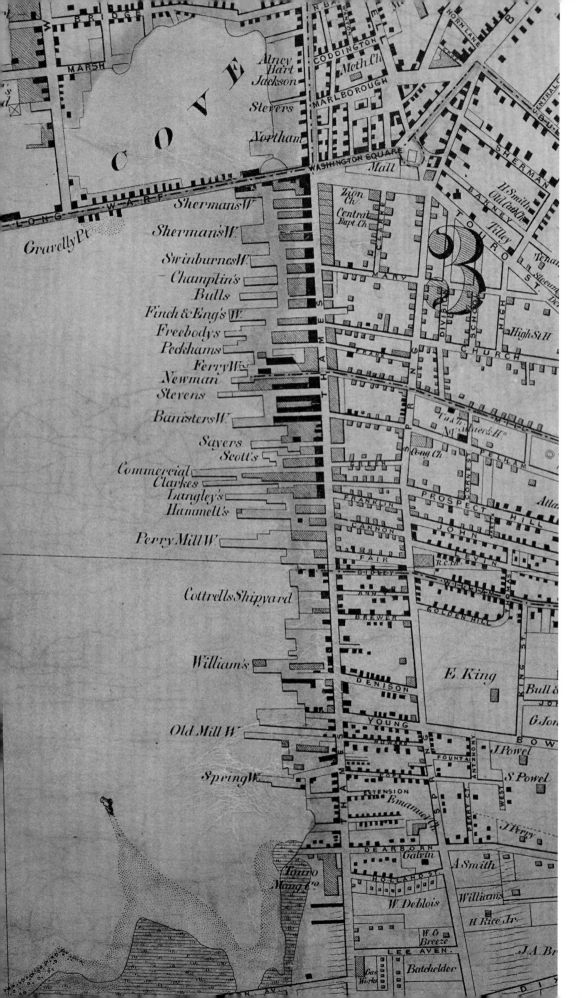

Fig. 66

Map of the Township of Newport and Middletown (detail of the wharves and Thames Street), from Sarony, Major and Knapp Lithographers, Coastal Survey Department, ca. 1860. Courtesy of Mr. & Mrs. S. Matthews V. Hamilton, Jr.

Fig. 67

Touro Street, ca. 1890, photograph. Newport
Historical Society, P5674.

The street is unpaved with cobbled borders. This was
the typical treatment of Newport streets until the late
nineteenth-century paving of the city's thoroughfares.

Fig. 68 *(left)*

Division Street, ca. 1885, photograph. Newport Historical Society, P5754.

Division Street is one of the best-preserved areas in the Historic Hill district. The buildings on its western side retain their eighteenth-century scale and lot sizes.

Fig. 69 *(below)*

Paving Thames Street, ca. 1910, photograph. Newport Historical Society, P9073_NDN 1109.

Fig. 70

The wharves of Thames Street in winter, ca. 1880,
photograph. Newport Historical Society, P9578.

Fig. 71

The Cooke House, ca. 1930, photograph. Newport Historical Society, P5424.

This mid-eighteenth-century house, once located at the corner of Thames and Green Streets, retained its original door and roofline with the addition of late nineteenth-century shop windows, the fate of many colonial period buildings on Thames Street. It was moved to Bannister's Wharf during urban renewal in the late 1960s and early 1970s.

Fig. 72 *(left)*

Thames Street, ca. 1890, photograph.
Newport Historical Society, P4176.

By the mid-nineteenth century, Thames Street
served as the main shopping and commercial
area in Newport. Victorian buildings crowded
the thoroughfare. Expanding the street to
address ever-increasing traffic congestion
became a major point of both public debate
and professional design proposals from the
early 1900s through the mid-1960s.

Fig. 73 *(above)*

The Bijou Theatre and Army Navy YMCA
on Thames Street, ca. 1910, photograph.
Newport Historical Society, P5654.

Fig. 74

Spring Street, ca. 1890, photograph. Newport Historical Society, P9416.

View of the John Banister House (ca. 1760). The street is depicted before the installation of electric streetcar railway tracks in 1889.

Fig. 75

Townsend's Hotel, Thames Street, ca. 1850, print. Newport Historical Society, 2004.13.126.

Several hotels appeared in Newport in the early 1840s. Townsend's Hotel served the commercial purposes of Thames Street while the Atlantic and Ocean House Hotels on Bellevue Avenue catered to summer visitors.

TOWNSEND'S HOTEL,
NEWPORT, R.I.

Fig. 76

Thames Street, ca. 1890, photograph. Newport
Historical Society, P1197.

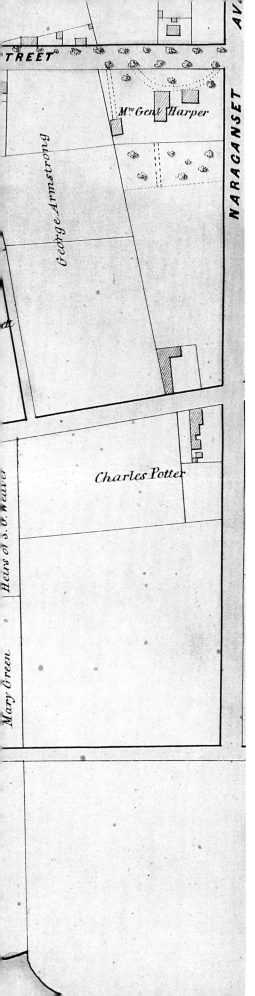

Fig. 77

Detail of lower Thames Street, ca. 1850. Newport Historical Society, from Matthew Dripps and B.I. Tilley, *Map of the City of Newport* (New York and Newport, RI, 1859). Newport Historical Society.

Thames Street is populated by commercial wharves and small lots for houses, while Bellevue Avenue, listed on this map as "Bellevue Street," is marked by early summer estates, such as that of George Noble Jones of Savannah.

Wharves still dominated in this part of the city, with the name of each proprietor clearly indicated on atlas maps (Figs. 77–83). But new technologies also made their presence felt in the complexes for the Newport Water Works and the Newport Gas Company on Thames Street, as well as the creation of the Fifth Ward district with standardized small house lots for the city's growing sector of workers (Figs. 84–86).

Technological progress quickened the pace of life, but the major industrialization and catastrophic fires that had transformed many urban centers bypassed Newport, leaving the historic core of the community largely intact. Artists discovered, venerated, and celebrated the picturesque quality of the colonial district, encompassing Washington Square, the adjacent Historic Hill, and the wharves of Thames Street. While some saw the timeworn buildings as urban dereliction, artists viewed them with aesthetic delectation.

Fig. 78

Lower Thames Street, from G. M.
Hopkins, *City Atlas of Newport,
Rhode Island* (Philadelphia,
1876). Newport Historical Society.
Photography courtesy of the
Preservation Society of Newport
County.

The southern portion of Thames Street
displays the increasing infill of this
commercial sector with homes for
workers. Charles Russell, a major real
estate developer, subdivided his land
for modest size house lots for workers.

Fig. 79 *(following page)*

Lower Thames Street and Bellevue
Avenue, from G. M. Hopkins, *City
Atlas of Newport, Rhode Island*
(Philadelphia, 1876). Newport
Historical Society. Photograph
courtesy of the Preservation Society
of Newport County.

Two forces influenced the development
of Newport in the mid-nineteenth
century: first, the commercial and
industrial activities of the waterfront,
and second, the rise of the city as a
fashionable summer resort.

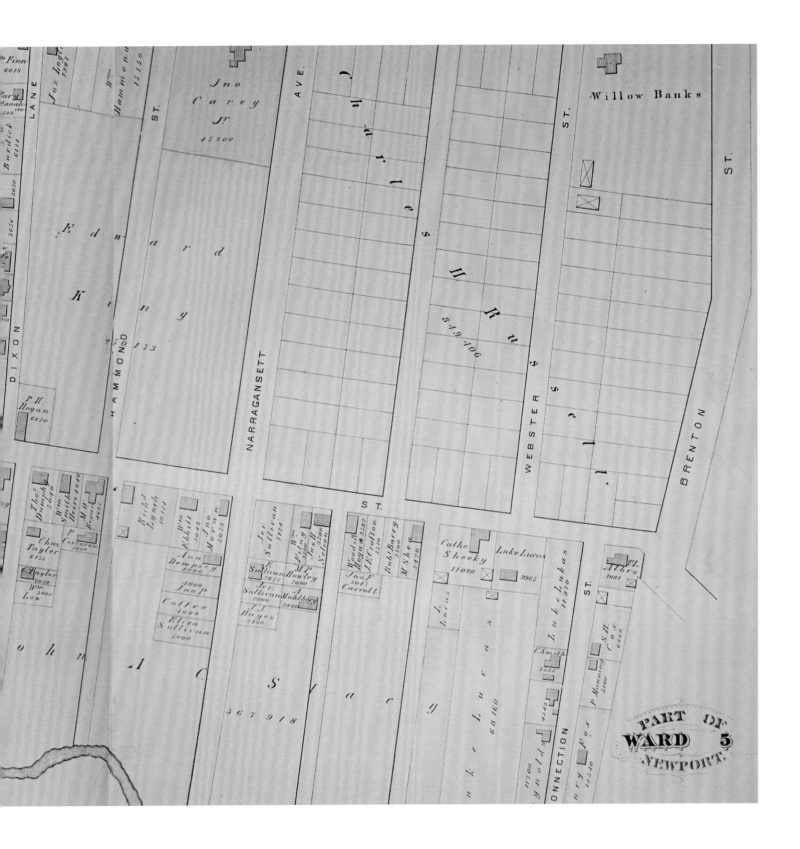

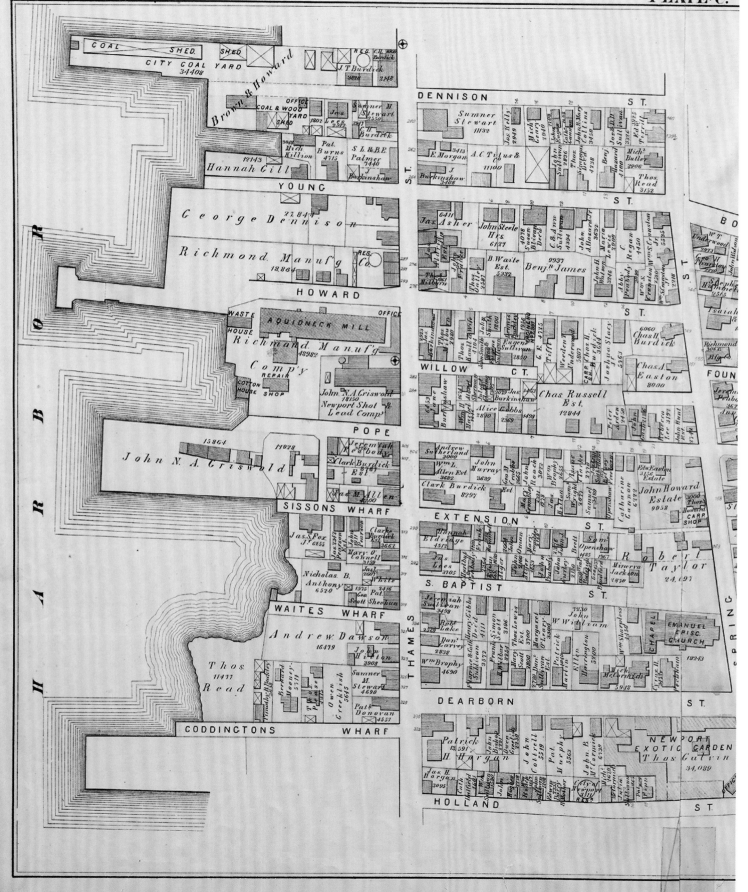

ATLANTIC
HOUSE

R. R. Hazard
53027

CORNE ST.

MARTIN ST.

JOHN ST.

LEVIN ST.

WILLIAM ST.

GOLDEN HILL ST.

THOMAS ST.

SPRING ST.

BOWERY ST.

KING ST.

JONES ST.

BELLEVUE

AVE

ST. MARY'S
ROMAN CATHOLIC
CHURCH
33632

ST. MARY'S
SCHOOL

CLIFTON
BURIAL
GROUND
9970

GREEN HOUSE

Edward
King
3709

Marietta

Sidney Brooks

Stevens

102,713

117,623

Edward King

346,000

Wm. H. King
144010

4

5

2nd Baptist
Society

Jos. Paddock
Heirs
19905

Devisees of
Kath Ruggles
17820

BELLEVUE AVE.
HOTEL 3900
Carl Hertzgen
BELLEVUE AVE.
GARDEN

Fig. 80 *(previous page)*

Summer estates on Bellevue Avenue, from G. M. Hopkins, *City Atlas of Newport, Rhode Island* (Philadelphia, 1876). Newport Historical Society. Photograph courtesy of the Preservation Society of Newport County.

Principles of the picturesque, most notable in the form of serpentine paths, dominate in the plans of the earliest Newport summer villas of the 1840s, the houses of Edward King and William Henry King.

Fig. 81

View of the cove, ca. 1890, photograph. Newport Historical Society, P8000.

Fig. 82

View of the Thames Street wharves toward Goat
Island, ca. 1880, photograph. Newport Historical
Society, P142.

Fig. 83

View of Goat Island (right) and Fort Adams in the distance (left) from the Thames Street wharves, ca. 1870, photograph. Newport Historical Society, P151.

Fig. 84 *(opposite)*

Lower Thames Street, from L. J. Richards and Co., *Atlas of the City of Newport* (Springfield, MA, 1907). Newport Historical Society.

The density of the lower Thames Street area increased dramatically by the early twentieth century. Wharves were adapted for emerging technologies, such as the Marine Railway, Staples Coal, and the Old Colony Street Railway Illumination Department.

Fig. 85

A changing streetscape on Thames Street, ca. 1870, photograph. Newport Historical Society, P1031.

Victorian (left), colonial (center), and Greek Revival (right) buildings created a complex, layered architectural scene on Thames Street by the mid-nineteenth century.

Fig. 86

Thames Street, ca. 1885, photograph. Newport Historical Society, P5320.

Fig. 87

William James Stillman, The Dunbar House with
the Colony House cupola in the background, 1874,
photograph. McKim Portfolio, Newport Historical
Society, P379.

Charles Follen McKim commissioned the
photographer William James Stillman to produce
a series of photographs on Newport's eighteenth-
century buildings, streetscapes, and decorative objects.
McKim's interest focused primarily on the vernacular
architecture of the city, with an emphasis on the
irregular rooflines and wings of colonial structures.

In the early 1870s, the architect Charles Follen
McKim played a significant role in cultivating interest
in the old quarter by commissioning photographs of
colonial era buildings, streetscapes, furniture, and
objects. His choice of subject matter is exceptional
for the period, for he did not always select famous
landmarks for inclusion in his study (Figs. 87–89).
Instead, his photographer, William James Stillman,
focused on the rambling rooflines and service wings
of colonial houses.[21] These appealed to McKim's
interest in picturesque outlines to inspire the new

Fig. 88

William James Stillman, View of Bridge Street, 1874,
photograph. McKim Portfolio, Newport Historical
Society, P393.

Fig. 89

William James Stillman, The backyard of a colonial
era house, 1874, photograph. McKim Portfolio,
Newport Historical Society, P394.

Charles Follen McKim was intrigued by the irregular
rooflines of vernacular colonial architecture in
Newport.

NEWPORT: THE ARTFUL CITY

style of houses he was designing in the aptly named "modernized colonial" manner. The architect was not primarily an antiquarian set on documenting the history of Newport's historic buildings. He used old forms and ornamental details to conjure up architectural fantasies for a new age. Writers also projected their own fantasies onto Newport, seeing what they wished to see. Among the most prominent was Henry James, the acclaimed novelist who knew Newport well from his time as a young man when he and his family resided in the city. Throughout many of his writings, James used the backdrops of buildings and their interiors to inform and reinforce his plots. He was also noted for his travel writings, capturing the geography, architecture, and culture of the places he visited. Both his sense of story line and setting converge in his writing on Newport, in which he cast the heart of the city in an ancient guise (Figs. 90 and 91):

> I have been quite awe-struck by the ancient State House [the Colony House of 1739–41] that overlooks the ancient Parade, an edifice ample, majestic, archaic, of the finest proportions and full of a certain public Dutch dignity. ... Here was the charming impression of a treasure of antiquity ... the wide, cobbly, sleepy space ... in the shadow of the State House, must have been much more of a Van der Heyden, or somebody of that sort than one could have dreamed.[22]

Henry James and other artists imposed their romantic views onto the city while, in the early

Fig. 90 *(opposite)*

Buildings near the historic spring, ca. 1880, photograph. Newport Historical Society, P9546.

This view includes the corner of the Colony House (left), the First Baptist Church (center), and an eighteenth-century house (right) all located near the spring, one of the earliest areas of colonial settlement. The house was demolished in the early 1900s.

1900s, the realities of Newport's antiquated (or complete lack of) infrastructure came into sharper focus. Urban planners were summoned to Newport in an attempt to solve an age-old problem, traffic circulation (Fig. 92). The narrow thoroughfares of the city center could not accommodate the pressure of that new mode of transportation, the automobile. The Newport Improvement Association, formed in 1912, commissioned the firm of Olmsted Brothers to study the urban plan with the aim of integrating the past with the present. Frederick Law Olmsted Jr. took a very different approach than many writers and painters, who tended to focus on the mood and atmosphere of the place. While Olmsted valued beauty, he integrated aesthetic with pragmatic solutions. He had a task to perform. In 1913, he produced *Proposed Improvements for Newport*, incorporating both aesthetic and functional values in a scheme to preserve and modernize the city.[23]

Fig. 91

Newport scene, 1906, postcard. Newport Historical
Society, 2010.26.1.

A postcard illustrating popular sites associated with
Newport's colonial history.

Fig. 92

Horses and carriages on Washington Square,
ca. 1900, postcard. Newport Historical Society, P9590.

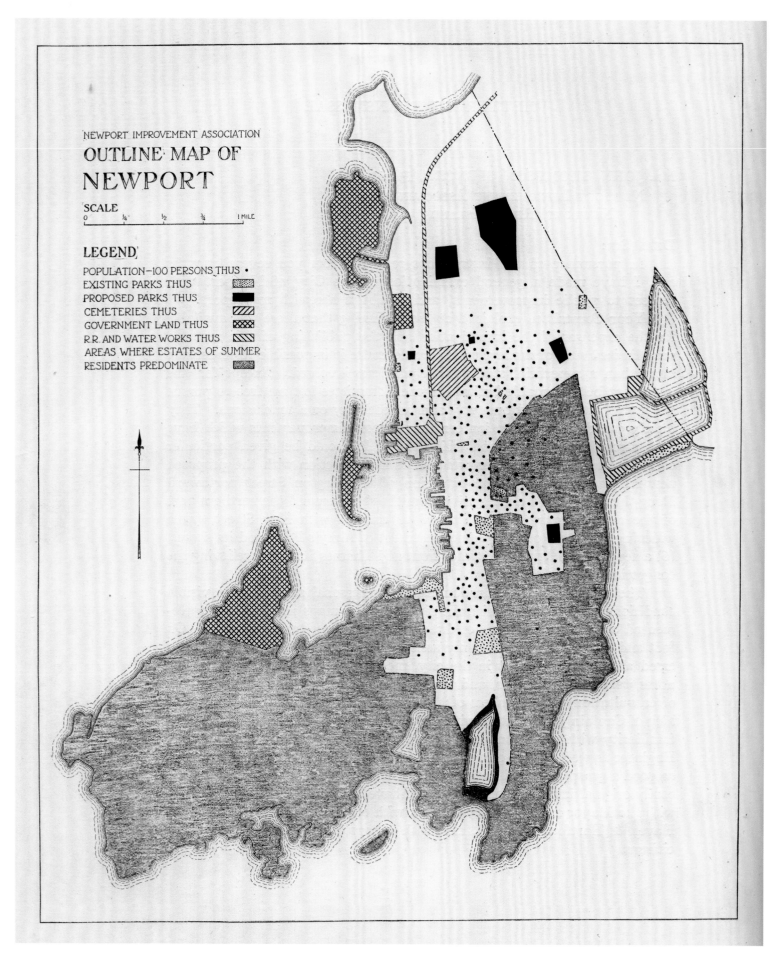

NEWPORT IMPROVEMENT ASSOCIATION

OUTLINE MAP OF
NEWPORT

SCALE

0   ¼   ½   ¾   1 MILE

LEGEND

POPULATION—100 PERSONS THUS ·
EXISTING PARKS THUS
PROPOSED PARKS THUS
CEMETERIES THUS
GOVERNMENT LAND THUS
R.R. AND WATER WORKS THUS
AREAS WHERE ESTATES OF SUMMER
RESIDENTS PREDOMINATE

Fig. 93 *(opposite)*

Frederick Law Olmsted Jr., *Proposed Improvements for Newport*, 1913. Newport Historical Society.

Olmsted's proposed improvements included a comprehensive study of the key features of Newport's urban plan, including railroads and waterworks, population density, and cemeteries and parks, both existing and proposed.

The character of entire streetscapes and the needs of traffic management were sensitively combined in a comprehensive study, which would be the first by many architects and urban planners throughout the twentieth century.

The tension between preserving historic character and introducing modern amenities formed the core of the Olmsted study, which provided a series of photographs of the city center with recommendations on care and conservation of historic structures and trees. There were schemes for major thoroughfares, including a widened Thames Street in order to address increasing street congestion at a time when horses and carriages shared space with streetcars, bicycles, and automobiles. Olmsted's introductory essay in the report assessed both positive and negative aspects of the urban fabric and outlined the features he believed made the city a viable entity (Fig. 93):

I was impressed anew with the picturesque charm of Newport. This is certainly not a startling discovery or an original observation, but I want to make it clear that I do not say it lightly … this picturesque quality of the city is a man-made affair, even though based on favorable natural opportunities and even though not deliberately planned. Its loss, if it is to be lost, will just as certainly be due to the action and the neglect of the people of the city.[24]

Olmsted treated Newport as a complete artistic and living entity in an approach to urban planning that incorporated the need for the preservation of historic structures and scenic vistas along with schemes for more efficient traffic patterns. The Olmsted family were well acquainted with the city. Frederick Law Olmsted Sr. was a legendary figure in American landscape design, integrating parks and parkways into city plans, most notably with the greensward system known as the "Emerald Necklace" in Boston.[25] While Olmsted Sr. did work on two Newport estates and Morton Park, his sons, as the firm of Olmsted Brothers, completed over thirty projects in Newport.[26] Thus, the family made a major impact on the topography of the city. Frederick Law Olmsted Jr.'s improvement plan respected the past while attempting to direct the future. Although the Olmsteds' proposals were not implemented by the city, their identified challenges and far-thinking solutions preoccupied Newport for decades and still remain relevant today.

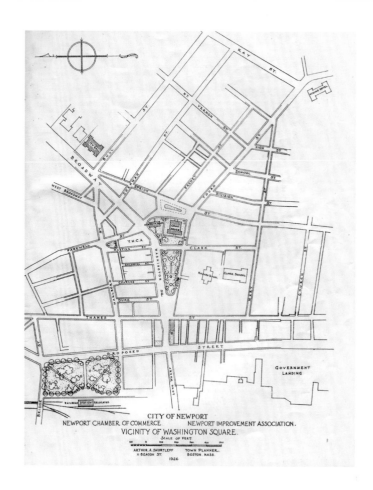

The question of how to adapt the historic downtown to modern needs came up again in 1926 when the city of Newport and the Newport Improvement Association hired the Boston town planner and landscape architect Arthur A. Shurtleff to address urban design issues. In his proposal, Shurtleff wrote, "Unlike the aim of an industrial city, Newport's chief ambition should be to preserve the scenic beauty of its environs, the attractiveness of its private places, the pleasantness of its streets, and the quaintness and charm of its closely built up district."[27] In the section of his report entitled "The Purpose of Town Planning," he warned against haphazard development and compromising the historic character of the downtown:

Newport is changing with new methods of transportation, new builders of small homes, new methods of store keeping, new kinds of occupations, coupled with new tastes in architecture. Unless these inevitable changes are guided in an intelligent way the city is in danger of losing its ancient charm and overriding the natural beauty of the open lands upon which its houses and streets are being built.[28]

Shurtleff emphasized the critical importance of preservation of the natural and human-made environment of Newport in a manner that may rightly be described as holistic (Figs. 94 and 95). His study encompassed the area of the spring at the juncture of Touro and Spring Streets, Washington Square, Long Wharf, and the railroad station

Fig. 94 *(above)*

Scheme for redesign of downtown Newport, from Arthur A. Shurtleff, *Regarding the Plans for the Growth of the City of Newport, RI* (January 20, 1926). Newport Historical Society.

Shurtleff's scheme for Newport respected the scale of the city's existing urban plan. He inserted a park in front of the railroad station yet kept his design within the confines of the historic street plan.

Fig. 95 *(opposite)*

Bird's-eye view of downtown Newport, from Arthur A. Shurtleff, *Regarding the Plans for the Growth of the City of Newport, RI* (1926). Newport Historical Society.

Shurtleff's bird's-eye view of the Washington Square area is an exercise in using historic scale in urban planning. Landmark buildings are clearly evident as character-defining features of the skyline. All other buildings are residential or commercial and of two to four stories.

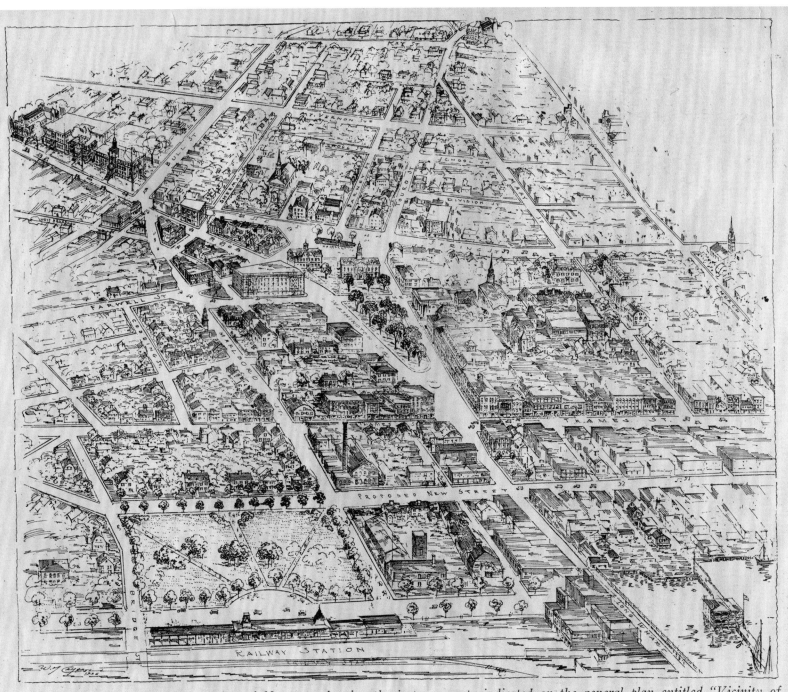

Bird's-eye view of the central portion of Newport showing the improvements indicated on the general plan entitled "Vicinity of Washington Square." In the foreground is seen the railway station and proposed adjacent park, the proposed new street giving frontage upon this park and affording relief to Thames Street congestion, the development of Washington Square, and the extension of Sherman Street, Clarke Street, and other streets of this vicinity.

on Bridge Street. Shurtleff provided a street plan
and a bird's-eye view to serve as a measure of
the appropriate scale of buildings in the district.
This approach built on the legacy of the Olmsted
improvement plan in its focus on integrating modern
efficiency with existing urban fabric, but Shurtleff
also had to address the increasing use of automobiles
as a primary mode of transportation in the 1920s.
His proposals introduced accommodation for cars
that exceeded those of the Olmsted plan of thirteen
years earlier:

> *The widening of Long Wharf should continue
> ... in order to provide a thoroughfare of
> sufficient width for the modern needs of
> Newport ... a roadway is greatly needed
> around the margins of the ancient wharves
> which form the southerly boundary of Long
> Wharf at its westerly end. A circuit highway
> of this kind would enhance the value of the
> property within the circuit and would also
> form an attractive sight-seeing route for
> persons wishing to view the harbor from one
> of its most sightly vantage points.*[29]

Shurtleff did not advocate for the waterfront park
recommended by the Olmsteds, but he foresaw
the potential of the area as a tourist destination
(Fig. 96). In its long history from the colonial period
to the early twentieth century, the waterfront served
as a commercial entity first and foremost. Artists
appreciated the timeworn atmosphere of decaying
eighteenth-century houses and service buildings
crowding the wharves, but the function of this
district was directed to business, and sightseers
generally flocked to the beaches, cliffs, and drives
along the sea on the eastern and southern sides
of the city. Neither proposals by Shurtleff nor the

Fig. 96 *(opposite)*

Long Wharf, ca. 1880, photograph. Newport Historical Society, P5994.

Fig. 97 *(above)*

Navy supply stores on Washington Square with a view to the Colony House, ca. 1960, photograph. Newport Historical Society, P8659.

Fig. 98 *(above right)*

Corner of Washington Square and Thames Street, 1963, photograph. Estate of Lloyd Robinson, Newport Historical Society, P8852.

Olmsteds were adopted, but they were portents of the future, raising the issues of traffic, appropriate business development, and the preservation of scenery and historic architecture that would eventually drive the renewal of Newport. In 1928, Shurtleff was appointed chief landscape architect for Williamsburg, Virginia. Newport, however rich in historic structures, would not follow the example of Williamsburg as a museum city. It would take another direction as the twentieth century unfolded.

By the 1950s, neon signs illuminated the restaurants, bars, navy supply stores, and small shops of Washington Square, Long Wharf, and Thames Street (Figs. 97 and 98). While change was ever present, some things stayed the same. The original street plan remained intact and the architectural landmarks of Trinity Church, Colony House, Touro Synagogue, and Brick Market remained constant anchors in the cityscape. The core of Newport,

Fig. 99

The Cooke House at the corner of
Thames and Green Streets, 1955,
photograph. Newport Historical
Society, P5425.

This colonial era house went through
several phases as a residence, then
a business, with accompanying
modifications through the centuries.
This was the fate of many eighteenth-
century buildings along Thames Street
as commercial activities increased in
the nineteenth century.

however, began to decay at an increasing rate as the
century reached its halfway mark. In the 1950s, when
the aesthetics of modernism honored immaculate
minimalism over the picturesque shabbiness of
historic buildings, Washington Square and the aging
wharves of Thames Street appeared outdated and
outmoded (Fig. 99). The proposals of the Olmsteds
and Shurtleff reappeared in a new guise when the
Newport Daily News reported, "Newport's often
advocated waterfront street paralleling Thames Street
may become a reality."[30] Such dreams of redesign
and renewal remained unrequited for yet another
decade due to lack of funds and consensus among the
community about the direction to take on the future
appearance of the city.

In the 1960s, the physical reinvention of Newport
became a dream finally realized for some and
an apocalyptic nightmare for others. Advocates
of modernist urban renewal called for a city of
progress and efficiency. There were, however, those
voices of nineteenth-century artists, historians, and
antiquarians speaking out from the past. Their work
in highlighting the significance of Newport's colonial
heritage eventually resulted in the creation of the
Newport Historic District in 1965. The protected
area encompassed all of Washington Square, the
Historic Hill, and the eastern side of Thames Street,
which were saved from the wrecking ball and not

included in redevelopment schemes. Change came to the old quarter, but it had to work in and around the city's architectural heritage.

Funding from the federal government for urban renewal in the mid-1960s initiated a new era of major redevelopment and construction in cities across the United States. Its effect on Newport's colonial quarter was nothing short of convulsive. In its entire history, Newport was subject to subdivision and expansion, but not to whole-scale demolition and redesign. In 1966, all of the lands not in the declared Newport Historic District, those parcels from the western side of Thames Street to the sea, were demolished to accommodate the four-lane road known as America's Cup Avenue, which cut across Long Wharf, separating it from its centuries-old connection with Washington Square. The historic buildings on Long Wharf and wharves on the waterfront from Brick Market to lower Thames Street were entirely eradicated to make way for modern development (Figs. 100–3).

Fig. 100 *(opposite)*

The west facade of Brick Market before redevelopment, ca. 1967, photograph. Rhode Island Collection, Providence Public Library, VM013_GF4751.

The eighteenth-century, gambrel-roofed house to the south (right) of the Brick Market was demolished during the major clearance of the area in the late 1960s as part of urban renewal.

Fig. 101 *(right)*

Demolition of buildings on Long Wharf and creation of the embankment to its south (right) for Perrotti Park, ca. 1967, photograph. Rhode Island Collection, Providence Public Library, VM013_GF4750.

Fig. 102

Demolition of buildings on Long Wharf, ca. 1967, photograph. Rhode Island Collection, Providence Public Library, VM013_GF4759.

Fig. 103

Aerial view of Newport after redevelopment, 1975, photograph. John T. Hopf Collection, Newport Historical Society, P8038.

The historic waterfront was demolished to accommodate the four-lane America's Cup Avenue with new buildings at either side. Perrotti Park rose on the embankment created from the zone once occupied by eighteenth- and nineteenth-century wharves. From 1966 to 1970, the urban renewal of this area of Newport was the most radical in the city's history.

Case Study #2

African American and Immigrant Populations in Early Newport

EDWARD E. ANDREWS, PhD

ASSOCIATE PROFESSOR AND CHAIR OF THE DEPARTMENT
OF HISTORY AND CLASSICS, PROVIDENCE COLLEGE

Charles Blaskowitz, *Plan of the Towne of Newport* (list of major buildings), 1777. Library of Congress.

THERE IS A BEAUTIFUL, DETAILED MAP OF Newport, Rhode Island, that was illustrated by a mapmaker named Charles Blaskowitz in 1777. Like most visual representations of early modern spaces, Blaskowitz's project lays out the key urban features of one of the most important cities in the early modern Atlantic world. Viewing the seaport from above, one can spy not only jutting wharves and active commercial districts, but also the specific street names that led directly to them, intimately connecting people's homes with the commercial activities on the water. The legend for the map notes some of the most important physical locales in the city, nodding to commercial and political spaces like the Brick Market and the Colony House, as well as other buildings like libraries, courthouses, and even a jail. But the majority of the items in the legend identify religious buildings, which makes sense for a seaport that had its historic roots in the principle of freedom of

References.

A *Trinity Church.*
B *1st Congregational Meeting House.*
C *2d Congregational Meeting House.*
D *1st Baptist Meeting House.*
E *2d Baptist Meeting House.*
F *3d Sabbatarian Baptist Meeting House.*
G *4th Baptist Meeting House.*
H *Friends Meeting House.*
I *Unitas Fratrum Meeting.*
K *Jews Synagogue.*
L *Court House.*
M *Goal.*
N *Alms & Work Houses.*
O *Redwoods Library.*
P *An Estate the Donation of Nathanl. Kay late Collector of his Majesty's Customs for the Support of an Assistant Minister in Trinity Church & Schooling Ten poor Boys.*
Q *Town School House.*
R *Market Houses.*
S *Rope Walks.*
T *A Battery raised by the Americans.*

112

conscience. If this map makes one thing clear, it's that Newport was born from the collision of two forces: water and worship.

But, like most maps, Blaskowitz's representation is illuminating and obscuring, insightful and incomplete. For while the map privileges the religious makeup of the city of Newport, it is silent on the groups that could not be represented neatly by an institutional mark. In fact, by the time that Blaskowitz fashioned the map, in the heat of the American Revolution, Newport was a remarkably diverse city. It was, for sure, filled with Anglicans and English Dissenters alike, but it also held a small German Moravian community, whose only mark on the map was for the "Unitas Fratrum Meeting." On the wharves and walkways in the eighteenth century there were also French Huguenot migrants, Africans and native-born African Americans (both free and enslaved), Sephardic Jews, as well as indigenous servants and enslaved peoples. And just as Blaskowitz was drawing this map, these local Newporters were joined by an occupying British force that brought with them German-speaking Hessian mercenaries, who themselves would later be replaced by French allies when the combat moved south. So, as alluring as it is, Blaskowitz's map displays a static, institutionalized version of Newport that belies its rich and ever-changing, mobile population. It is, in some ways, a two-dimensional vision of a four-dimensional reality.

Although Newport is often noted for being officially "settled" in 1639, the English Dissenters who established it as a permanent town were not the first humans to migrate there. In fact, Narragansett Indians travel frequently for seasonal fishing, and the entire region around the now-named Narragansett Bay was a kind of borderland among Pokanoket, Narragansett, and Wampanoag groups that harvested its fish and fowl and competed for the nutrient-rich agricultural lands along the bay's shorelines.

Those rich shorelines attracted English settlers as well, led by a group of migrants escaping persecution in Massachusetts. This became a consistent thread in Newport's history, and very early on two other immigrant groups in particular would migrate to the growing town and contribute to its culture, politics, and economy. First, the Society of Friends, also known as the Quakers, found in Newport a safe haven in the 1660s in which they could build a successful community. By 1700, they had established a meetinghouse, which still stands at the corners of today's Farewell Street, Marlborough Street, and Dr. Marcus Wheatland Boulevard. The Newport meetinghouse would become an epicenter of Quaker activity, and Quakers emerged as key leaders in both municipal and colonial government throughout the seventeenth and eighteenth centuries.

Sephardic Jews were another major group to land in Newport. They traced their roots back to the Jewish expulsion of the Spanish Reconquista and then to the ever-changing imperial jockeying that rocked the early modern Atlantic world. Jewish migrants came to Newport from the Caribbean in the wake of seventeenth-century wars between the various imperial powers. In Newport, these groups found enough stability to set down permanent roots, purchase a burial ground, and by 1763, open the region's first synagogue, a beautiful Palladian building designed by an increasingly popular architect named Peter Harrison.

Quakers and Jews were, like the dissenting groups that "settled" Newport, diasporic people, constantly escaping persecution in an age of imperial tumult. On the one hand, Newport was far from an idyllic paradise for these migrants. Proximity to Puritan colonies and persistent challenges to their religion were of paramount concern to Quakers, and Jews possessed limited political rights and were barred from the upper echelons of government. Still, later Quakers such as Abraham Redwood and Jews like Jacob Rodriguez Rivera and Aaron Lopez were able to amass incredible fortunes due to the increasing integration of Newport into the Atlantic world economy. As the best and southernmost harbor for New England, the seaport emerged as a crucial local go-between for the growing cities of Boston and New York; by the second quarter of the eighteenth century, Newport was as a major economic player in its own right. It would be a key exporter of timber, candles, and, famously, rum. At the same time, however, the increasing integration into the Atlantic world also meant that Newport played an inordinately large role in one of its biggest tragedies: the transatlantic slave trade.

Historical institutions, scholars, journalists, and other public figures have been working hard to correct the popular notion that slavery was only a Southern problem. Indeed, slavery had deep roots in the city of Newport and helped to grow the city from a small town on the southern edge of New

England into a major transatlantic seaport. Slavery had long been part of Rhode Island's history; even in the late seventeenth century, the local government passed a law that tried to prohibit its citizens from their frequent practice of purchasing Africans in bondage. By the middle of the eighteenth century, local censuses showed that nearly 20 percent of the population was "Negro." These included, at first, enslaved peoples from the Caribbean. Increasingly, however, Newport's black population came directly on slave ships from Africa (although usually by way of the Caribbean).

The impact on Newport was profound. In 1758, when local minister Ezra Stiles drafted a manuscript map of the city, many of the wharves were named for captains and investors—Gardners, Wantons, Godfreys, and others—who plied the waters of the transatlantic slave trade (Fig. 21). "The first wheel of commerce," as historian Elaine Crane put it, slavery in Newport became the key factor through which the economic and urban development of the city accelerated. The commercial activity in the city center achieved such a furious pace that the government

Opposite

Bellevue Avenue (detail), ca. 1890, photograph. Clarence Stanhope Collection, Newport Historical Society, P739.

even imposed a three-pound tax on each enslaved person brought into the colony to help pay for paving and repairs of Newport's roads.

Historians often employ a distinction between "slave societies" and "societies with slaves" to classify a particular region's relationship with that deplorable institution. Clear examples of slave societies could be found in places like Jamaica, Barbados, and eventually Virginia, where the emergence of an agricultural society focused on a particular crop (e.g., sugar, tobacco) necessitated constant importation of African bodies, strict laws and draconian treatment, spectacles of violence against blacks, and often a black majority of slaves versus a smaller society of white overseers, which resulted in a kind of persistent paranoia among whites out of fear of insurrection. Societies with slaves, on the other hand, contained enslaved peoples, but slavery was one form of labor among many (including indentured servitude, apprenticeship, and free labor). In these societies, the relative proportion of enslaved peoples was much lower.

Was Newport a slave society? A society with slaves? It's difficult to say, and the answer depends on *when*. Even when speaking about the middle of the eighteenth century—the height of the horrible institution in the city—slavery within the city's bounds never achieved the kind of dominance it would achieve in other slave societies. A few households held more than five slaves, but according to a detailed 1774 census, most slaveholding households contained only one or two. And, instead of a focused monoculture, the evidence suggests that enslaved Africans in Newport did a range of things: they were bakers and shoe-shiners, they worked in rum distilleries and they oversaw shops, they were cordwainers, stonecutters, and masons. Their hands and their labor helped to construct iconic buildings—like the Colony House—that were resting near the newly paved streets that their bodies had paid for. And the slave laws that did emerge in Rhode Island focused mainly on *mobility*—punishing those who helped enslaved people escape on a boat, for example—rather than on the threat of insurrection. So, on the ground, Newport looks very much like a society with slaves. And yet, the fact that its economy was so rooted in the slave trade suggests an even more complicated story. It may not have been a slave society like Barbados or Virginia, but it was dependent on the institution. Indeed, it's hard to imagine the city's history and development without it.

The American Revolution brought both challenges and opportunities for Newport's black community. Many blacks enlisted in the war effort as a way to attempt to achieve their freedom, while others used wartime chaos to run away. In the wake of the war, Rhode Island passed gradual emancipation laws and many slaveholders began to manumit their bondspeople. And yet, even after a revolution fought for principles of liberty and equality, slavery persisted and racism against free blacks was rampant.

Newport's black community responded to this racism in a variety of ways: considering the possibility of emigration to Africa, moving to new communities like Boston and Providence, founding schools for black children, and establishing benevolent organizations

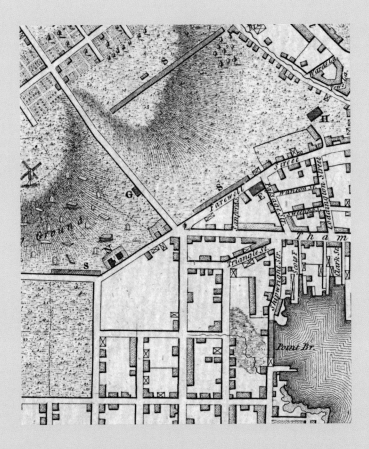

Charles Blaskowitz, *Plan of the Towne of Newport* (detail of the corner of Thames and Farewell Streets), 1777. Library of Congress.

for the welfare of their members. Some, like Newport Gardner, emerged as powerful black voices who purchased homes, built black neighborhoods, and fought against the structural and daily racism that plagued a city built in large part with proceeds from the African trade. In the 1820s, a small group of them, led by Gardner himself, migrated to the new black colony of Liberia. For them, freedom was to be found not in America, but in a precarious future in Africa. Sadly, many of them died soon after arrival. Those who remained behind continued to set down

their roots in Newport and build a black community that would shape the city's history to this day.

Just as many people of African descent were abandoning Newport, others were hastening to inhabit it. Perhaps the largest group among these in the years immediately after 1800 was the Irish, who came in the wake of the War of 1812 to work as laborers building Fort Adams. They established their own neighborhood, known as the Fifth Ward, between the town center and the fort, with a Roman Catholic church there as well. After the Civil War, a large number of immigrants from the South continued to build Newport's substantial community of people of African descent. Today, the city claims immigrants from all over the world.

Let us return to that beautiful Blaskowitz map. If one looks closely—really closely—at the map, one can find something interesting. It's a small vertical mark that represents a lonely tree in a deforested urban landscape, and it's located on the left edge of the map, at the corners of Farewell and Thames Streets, leading northward and out of the city. The tree isn't labeled. It doesn't seem to be near anything of significance. And yet, this was the very site of several cultural gatherings, which included not only patriotic protests and celebrations during the revolutionary era, but also seasonal African celebrations every June, which reinforced cultural ties to Africa and cultivated a sense of black identity in New England, even in the midst of racial slavery. The tree, represented only by that small vertical mark, is a small but important reminder of the role that all Newporters—free and enslaved, black and white—played in the city's history.

Burying Ground

Triangle st.

Shipwright Str.

Point T.

Clark St.

Marlborough Str.

Queen Hithe

Thames

R

Point Br.

Draw Brid.

Long Wharf

T

Romus Wh.

Wanton's Wh.

Ellery's Ferry Wh.

A PLAN of
the
TOWN OF NEWPORT
in
RHODE ISLAND.

Surveyed by CHARLES BLASKOWITZ,

Engraved and Publish'd

BY

WILLM. FADEN, Charing Cross Septr. 1st 1777.

Scale of Feet.

500   1,000   1,500

GOA

CHAPTER 2

THE POINT

The Intersection of Romance and Reality

The guiding philosophy of the Society of Friends, the dreams of nineteenth-century artists for a perceived colonial past, and the pragmatic business of transportation all converged on the Point, a neighborhood where reality and romance have intersected and intertwined for centuries. This district possesses one of the highest concentrations of pre-revolutionary houses in the United States. The color, texture, and materials of eighteenth-century buildings make this area a treasury of colonial domestic architecture in New England. Its streetscapes are also a complex layering of later additions, when parcels of land established in the colonial period were subdivided during the Victorian era.

The urban layout of the Point began with an ideal, the creation of a community expressing the values of the Society of Friends. While entrepreneurship dominated the general plan of Newport, the Point is a striking example of religious principles producing

At the head of yonder pristine wharf, in that spacious and still cheerful abode, dwell the beautiful Robinson sisterhood—the three Quaker belles of Revolutionary days, the memory of whose loves might lend romance to the neighborhood forever.

Thomas Wentworth Higginson
Oldport Days, 1873

a highly organized urban unit. Through a bequest by Nicholas Easton and his widow, Ann Bull Easton, lands on the point extending along the harbor and cove were acquired by the Society of Friends between 1674 and 1706.[31] By 1725, the Quakers of Newport directed their members to investigate the planning of Philadelphia by their brethren.[32] Unlike the economic impetus underlying the creation of Thames Street and the wharves, the organization of the Point, while conscious of commercial activities, exhibits the spiritual and cultural beliefs of the Quakers. Samuel Easton, a member of Newport's Society of Friends, laid out a symmetrical grid pattern (Fig. 104) with parcels of relatively equal size and street names based on numbers and trees.[33] This formula, with its emphasis on order, equality, and modesty, is similar to that set forth by William Penn for Philadelphia (1682), where the distinctly North American habit of naming streets after trees developed and spread across the nation. Elm, Poplar, Willow, Walnut, and Chestnut Streets (Fig. 105), all running in an east–west orientation, attest to this trend in the Point. It would have been viewed as vanity to name a street after a person. Water Street, extending the full length of the shoreline, was only retitled as Washington Street after the War of Independence, when the Quaker presence was less dominant. The grid layout also derives from the classical principles of European town planning developed during the Renaissance. This ancient Greek urban model appeared during the Hellenistic age in cities such as Miletus and Priene.[34] Romans in turn adapted the grid to both military camps and newly founded cities throughout

their empire. As Renaissance scholars and artists rediscovered the art and cultural achievements of the classical world, the grid pattern became the ideal for urban planning. With its emphasis on order and function and its appeal to reason, the grid crossed the Atlantic and was utilized in Spanish and French colonies, such as Quito (1534) in Ecuador and Louisbourg (c. 1720) in Canada. In British North America, the grid was applied in fully developed formats for entire cities and towns such as nearby Bristol, Rhode Island (1680), which belonged to the Massachusetts Bay Colony until the mid-eighteenth century, and Williamsburg, Virginia (1699).[35] The Quakers of Newport, while learned and possibly aware of ancient traditions in urban design, most likely valued the grid more for its practicality and simplicity rather than its classical allusions.

The houses, docks, and warehouses of leading merchants lined the west-facing waterfront on the aptly named Water Street, while the shops of cabinetmakers and artisans, such John Goddard, John and Christopher Townsend, and Henry Belcher, filled the inner blocks of the Point (Fig. 106). With land only a few feet above sea level, the area was bordered by marshland on the east, a large cove and Long Wharf creating the southern boundary, and a fortification known as the "Battery" to the north (Fig. 107).

During the course of the late eighteenth and nineteenth centuries, the original parcels of land on the Point, once containing three to five dwellings and large garden plots, were subdivided and built upon in prevailing Victorian styles, increasing the density and architectural variety of the streetscapes

Fig. 104 *(right)*

Samuel Easton, Map of Easton's Point (detail), 1725. Newport Historical Society.

The land is divided into equal parcels for sale. The names of owners are listed on each lot.

Fig. 105 *(below)*

Detail of streets on the Point named after trees, ca. 1850, from Matthew Dripps and B.I. Tilley, *Map of the City of Newport* (New York and Newport, RI, 1859). Newport Historical Society.

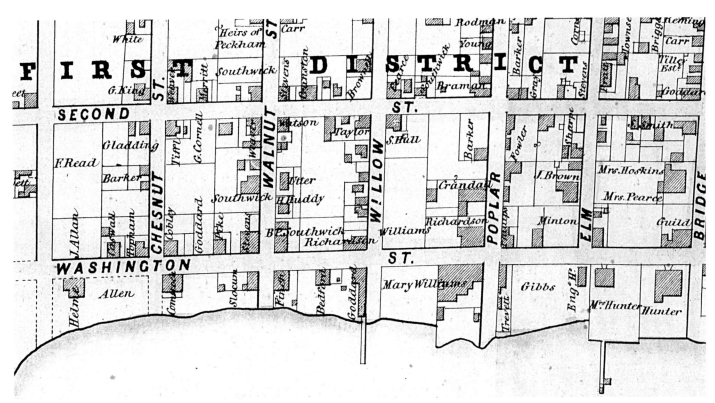

Fig. 106

Jonas Bergner, Bridge Street looking east to Thames Street, ca. 1890, photograph. Newport Historical Society, P9208.

The street retains its original eighteenth-century scale in buildings and layout.

Fig. 108 *(opposite below)*

The Point in the mid-nineteenth century, ca. 1850, from Matthew Dripps and B.I. Tilley, *Map of the City of Newport* (New York and Newport, RI, 1859). Newport Historical Society.

The original eighteenth-century lots on the Point were subdivided to accommodate the increased need for building.

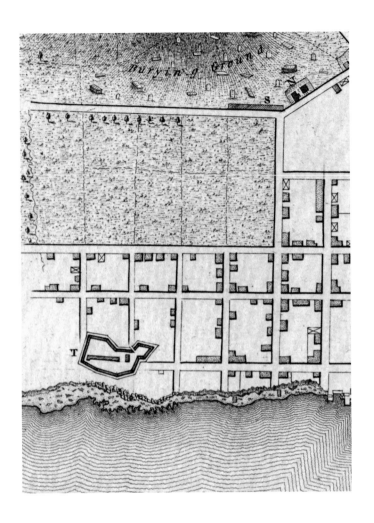

Fig. 107

Charles Blaskowitz, *Plan of the Towne of Newport* (detail of the Battery on the Point), 1777. Library of Congress.

(Figs. 108–11). As railroads traversed the nation in the mid-1800s, they made their arrival in Newport in February 1867 with the completion of the Old Colony Railroad, providing a station at Bridge Street and a terminus on Long Wharf (Figs. 112–16).[36] By 1907, the cove had been completely filled in (Fig. 117) and formed the nexus of an integrated transportation system connecting Newport by rail and steamship with nearby Fall River, Massachusetts, and Providence, Rhode Island, and, farther afield, New York City.[37]

Technological change impacted the Point, but it still retained its original street grid and eighteenth-century architecture. Amid new industrial progress, romantic visions arose in the minds of artists and writers who lived and wandered the streets of the neighborhood. Thomas Wentworth Higginson, a Unitarian minister, author, and friend and mentor to Emily Dickinson,

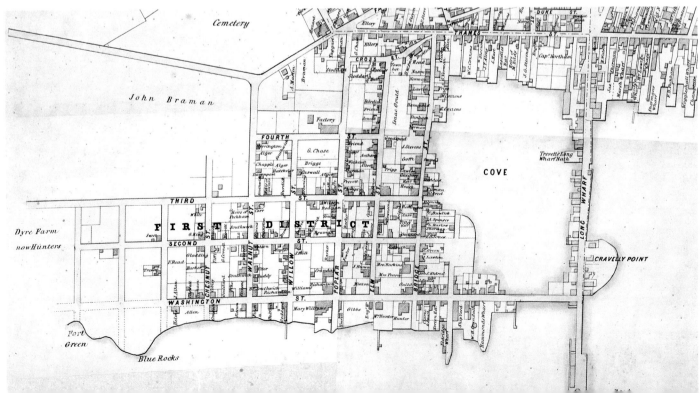

Fig. 109

A street on the Point, ca. 1880, photograph. Newport Historical Society, P5657.

Two colonial houses and a Greek Revival in the center illustrate the architectural evolution of the Point.

Fig. 110 *(opposite)*

The Point, from G. M. Hopkins, *City Atlas of Newport, Rhode Island* (Philadelphia, 1876). Newport Historical Society. Photograph courtesy of the Preservation Society of Newport County.

CITY OF NEWPORT
RHODE ISLAND

Parts & Wards 1 & 3

NEWPORT HARBOR

FAREWELL

BRAMAN CEMETERY COMPANY
142,177

Scale 100 Feet to the Inch.

REFERENCES

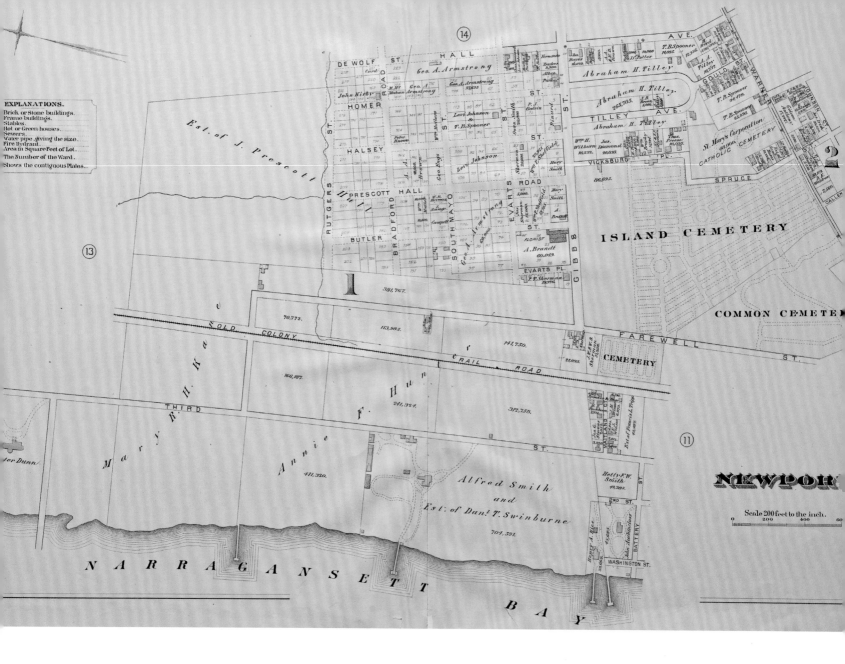

Scale 200 feet to the inch.

Fig. 111

The Point, from G. M. Hopkins, *City Atlas of Newport, Rhode Island* (Philadelphia, 1883). Newport Historical Society. Photograph courtesy of the Preservation Society of Newport County.

Farms, open meadowland, and country estates characterized the area at the northern perimeter of the Point. With the arrival of the Old Colony Railroad in the 1860s, commercial activity—and a growing population of workers to support it—increased on the Point. The Estate of J. Prescott Hall, owner of the country house known as Malbone, subdivided its lands near the Point into small lots of equal size to appeal to workers. Alfred Smith, Newport's leading real estate developer, also invested in waterfront property in the area.

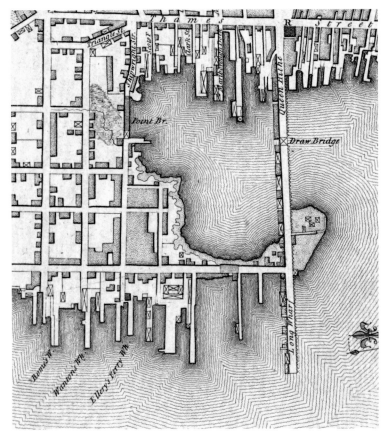

Fig. 113 *(above)*

Charles Blaskowitz, *Plan of the Towne of Newport* (detail of the Point), 1777. Library of Congress.

Fig. 114

Map of the Township of Newport and Middletown (detail of the cove and the Point), from Sarony, Major and Knapp Lithographers, Coastal Survey Department, ca. 1860. Courtesy of Mr. & Mrs. S. Matthews V. Hamilton, Jr.

Fig. 112

The cove and Long Wharf, ca. 1880, photograph. Gift of Lloyd A. Robinson, Newport Historical Society, P9543.

The main railroad station appears beyond the cove at the center of the photograph.

127

conjured up scenes on the Point, viewing the old neighborhood as a colonial era theater, of sorts:

Sometimes when I stand upon the pier by night, and look across the calm black waters ... I can imagine that I discern the French and English vessel just weighing anchor; I see de Lauzan and de Noailles embarking and catch the last sheen upon their lace, the last glitter of their swords.[38]

Higginson refers to the occupation of Newport by French troops in 1780, when the comte de Noailles was billeted at the house of Thomas Robinson

Fig. 115

Two boys by the waterfront looking across the cove from the railroad tracks toward the colonial houses of the Point, ca. 1880, photograph. Newport Historical Society, P8001.

(Fig. 118), whose daughters, as recorded both in letters and legend, became much admired as symbols of American naturalness and fresh beauty. The chevalier de Ternay, admiral of the French fleet, lived nearby at the Wanton residence. French officers

Fig. 116

Old Colony Railroad stop at Third Street on the
Point, ca. 1880, photograph. Newport Historical
Society, P8790.

lent an air of aristocratic glamour to the Point, which sparked the imaginations of late nineteenth-century artists. During the 1870s, the search for an American identity preoccupied many a painter, writer, and architect. They found their material inspiration in places dating to the colonial era. At the same time Higginson was inspired by the Point in his writing, the architect Charles Follen McKim became enamored of the neighborhood and, in 1872, began work on additions to the mid-eighteenth-century Robinson House.[39] McKim devised a Colonial Revival–style living space, referred to as a "keeping room," for the Robinson House and went

on to work across the street at the Dennis House (ca. 1750), providing modified doorway designs in a liberally interpreted pastiche of Georgian details. The result for any visitor walking the streets of the Point is to encounter both authentic and contrived colonial buildings that serve the purpose of whatever the individual seeks, whether historical accuracy or design fantasy, or both. There is something for everyone in the remaining layers of the past. Higginson cast such buildings, both grand and modest, as characters in *Oldport Days* (1873), in which he dwells on the passing of time in a country barely one hundred years old:

Fig. 117 *(opposite)*

View of the cove, ca. 1910, photograph. Newport Historical Society, P3038.

Fig. 118 *(below)*

The Robinson House on Washington Street, ca. 1880, photograph. Newport Historical Society, P4844.

By the mid- to late nineteenth century, Washington Street was lush with mature trees and the colonial houses had acquired a patina of age that so appealed to artists, architects, and writers with a taste for the romantic and picturesque.

Is it possible for an unpainted wooden building to assume, in this climate, a more time-worn aspect than that of any stone; and on these wharves everything is so old, and yet … you might fancy that the houses had been sent down there to play during their childhood, and that nobody had ever remembered to fetch them.[40]

Both architect and writer encountered a built environment that inspired their vision of a colonial heritage that was, for them, heroic in its historical events and sublime in its physical beauty. While Higginson and McKim were musing on aged wharves and houses on the western waterfront of the Point (Figs. 119–22), rail and steam were defining the eastern and southern borders of the district. This interplay of old and new, the undeniable fact of physical expansion and the visionary fiction of artistic production prompted by Newport's history and scenic beauty, would continue to play out as time marched on.

Fig. 120 *(above)*

The Point, ca. 1880, photograph.
Newport Historical Society, P8805.

Fig. 121 *(left)*

Waterside view of the Robinson
House, ca. 1900, photograph.
Clarence Stanhope Collection,
Newport Historical Society, P5694.

Fig. 122

The cove, ca. 1930, photograph. Newport Historical Society, P138.

The twentieth century greeted the Point in desperate circumstances. Rail and steam, which had made the district the most up-to-date transportation center, were outmoded by mid-century. Long Wharf, at the southern tip of the Point, was especially vulnerable. Its state of dereliction was undeniable (Figs. 123 and 124). In fact, the entire breadth of the colonial sector of Newport, encompassing the Point, Washington Square, Thames Street, the Historic Hill, and Broadway, were in physical and economic decay. Residents rose to the challenge with the creation of Operation Clapboard, a nonprofit organization formed to assist homeowners throughout Newport in the restoration of their

Fig. 123

Thomas T. Benson, Bridge Street, 1967, photograph. Gift of Operation Clapboard, Newport Historical Society, P9191.

Fig. 124

Houses on the Point, ca. 1880, photograph. Newport Historical Society, P8874.

Colonial houses, weathered but authentic, retaining their original rooflines, doors, and windows. Artists celebrated the faded buildings as remnants of a founding mythology of the American colonies.

Fig. 125

View of Goat Island, ca. 1915, photograph. Newport Historical Society, P9273.

During the mid-1800s, a series of houses with mansard roofs were constructed on Goat Island.

buildings. The Point still remained home to workers and artists who settled in the area, attracted by its historic appeal even before commencement of restoration efforts. Urban renewal in the mid-1960s, however, had the force of federal government funds and a preference for large-scale planning efforts rather than locally driven preservation schemes.

The new causeway to Goat Island, up to that point only accessible by boat, and the entire demolition of all structures on Long Wharf (Figs. 125–29) sparked a major controversy over the future of the district. If Bridge Street, as intended by the planners, was to serve as the access road to the causeway, the tone and life of the narrow streets of the Point would be adversely affected. With its eighteenth-century houses, Bridge Street preserved the scale and architectural integrity of its original creators. Residents called for nearby Marsh Street to be used as the access road to Goat Island. They were successful and the character of Bridge Street and the Point retained their historic integrity. No other urban renewal efforts focused on the Point. Its architectural rehabilitation would remain in the hands of private property owners. As a result, the Point today is a richly varied architectural ensemble with a Quaker-designed street plan and one of the largest concentrations of colonial era wooden structures in North America sharing space with later Victorian buildings.

Fig. 126 *(left)*

Goat Island, 1965, photograph. John T. Hopf Collection, Newport Historical Society, P9247.

Goat Island is occupied by facilities for the Torpedo Station. Long Wharf and the Old Colony Railroad tracks appear in the upper left.

Fig. 127 *(below left)*

Jerry Taylor, Derelict buildings on Goat Island, 1967, photograph. Newport Historical Society, P8058.

Fig. 128 *(opposite top)*

Areas marked for demolition and redevelopment in the mid-1960s during urban renewal, 1967, photograph. John T. Hopf Collection, Newport Historical Society, P5999.

Part of the scheme, not indicated on this photograph, was the creation of a causeway to link Goat Island with the Point.

Fig. 129 *(opposite below)*

Goat Island, from L. J. Richards and Co., *Atlas of the City of Newport* (Springfield, MA, 1907). Newport Historical Society. Photograph courtesy of the Preservation Society of Newport County.

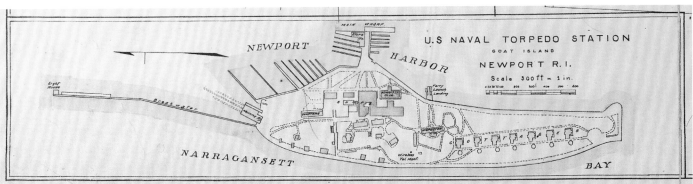

CHAPTER 3

A CITY BOTH PICTURESQUE AND GILDED

Bellevue Avenue, Ochre Point, and Ocean Drive

Picturesque Resort: 1840–90

THE ESTABLISHMENT OF BELLEVUE AVENUE and Ocean Drive, land subdivision, real estate speculation, and resort architecture dominated Newport's development as a seaside retreat in the mid-nineteenth through the early twentieth centuries. As the acknowledged "Queen of Resorts," the city experienced a flurry of construction as summer houses rose on the once open meadows to the east and south of the old colonial quarter.[41] Patrons and their designers in this era valued the picturesque, celebrating the type of spectacular natural landscape which Newport possessed in abundance. Fashionable society brought its own codes of conduct and behavior to this scenic spot, which evolved into a place combining social exclusivity with public display, where the desire to see and be seen dictated social habits and their settings. The function of the streetscapes would be

Newport is the most interesting of our summer colonies. Its newer portions show a characteristic instance of village planning which I have always spoken of as peculiarly American—wide streets of detached houses … all overshadowed by thickset and lofty trees.

Mariana Griswold Van Rensselaer
"American Country Dwellings,"
The Century Magazine, May 1886

Previous spread

Carriage on Bellevue Avenue, ca. 1905, photograph.
Newport Historical Society, P4163.

to both conceal and reveal, to tempt and taunt, with buildings produced by great wealth and purported taste intended to be glimpsed through wooden fences and wrought iron gates.

A dirt road, known as Jew Street, so named for the Jewish cemetery at its northern point, became the starting point for urban expansion in the 1850s. Leading south from the colonial quarter, the street opened onto pastureland with views to the distant harbor and ocean (Fig. 130). Speculators played a pivotal role in transforming large tracts of real estate in this area into a fashionable quarter. They

Fig. 130

Galt and Hoy, *Newport, RI* (New York, 1878).
Library of Congress, G3774.N4A3 1878 .G3.

This bird's-eye view of Newport emphasizes the importance of landscape and the sea. Rather than focusing, as with earlier maps, on the harbor and lands emanating from the waterfront, the Galt and Hoy view starts with the cliffs and seaside in the foreground and gives visual preeminence to the summer cottages of Bellevue Avenue and Ocean Drive. The heart of the colonial city is in the upper part of the view, literally the background. By 1878, the year of this view's production, Newport's role as a fashionable seaside resort is evident in the amount of real estate devoted to summer villas and the grand avenues providing for carriage rides to various scenic places.

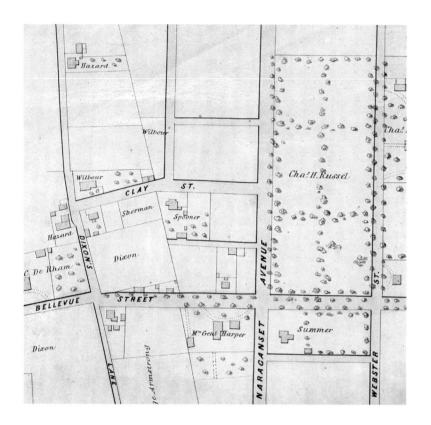

were assisted by George Champlin Mason, an artist, architect, and editor of the *Newport Mercury* who used the newspaper to promote the idea that the future of Newport lay in its role as a summer resort.[42] Central to this effort was the creation of a proper thoroughfare providing access to the cliffs and ocean on the eastern and southern portions of the city. Jew Street was extended and, when completed in 1853, given the official title of "Bellevue Avenue," or "beautiful view," a French name inspired, in part, by the grand boulevards of Paris and other major cities.[43] This long, straight road opened up the entire eastern side of Newport to development (Figs. 131–43). Farms were purchased and the land organized into parcels. Street plans in this district followed a symmetrical manner since the flat topography lent itself to orderly planning (Fig. 144).[44]

Fig. 131 *(above left)*

Newport in the mid-1800s, ca. 1850, from Matthew Dripps and B.I. Tilley, *Map of the City of Newport* (New York and Newport, RI, 1859). Newport Historical Society.

Bellevue Avenue, formally laid out and named in 1853, is listed on this map as "Bellevue Street."

Fig. 132 *(above right)*

Map of the Township of Newport and Middletown (detail of Bellevue Avenue), from Sarony, Major and Knapp Lithographers, Coastal Survey Department, ca. 1860. Courtesy of Mr. & Mrs. S. Matthews V. Hamilton, Jr.

With the completion of Bellevue Avenue in 1853, real estate developers, among them Alfred Smith, subdivided existing farmlands. By 1860, the majority of land in this relatively flat terrain was organized into regular parcels, new side streets were created, and the boom in summer cottage construction began in earnest.

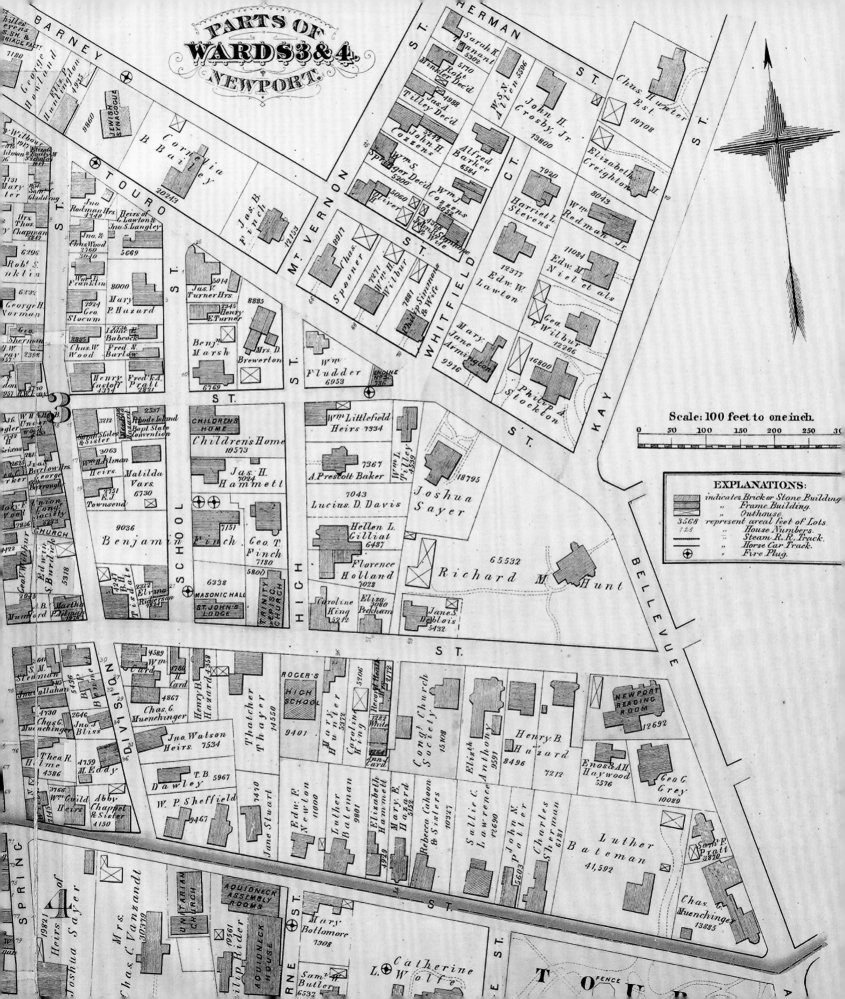

PARTS OF WARDS 3 & 4, NEWPORT.

HERMAN ST.

Scale: 100 feet to one inch.

0 50 100 150 200 250 30

EXPLANATIONS:
— indicates Brick or Stone Building
" " Frame Building
" " Outhouse
3568 represent areal feet of Lots
125 " House Numbers.
" Steam R.R. Track.
" Horse Car Track.
⊕ " Fire Plug.

Fig. 133 *(previous page)*

Bellevue Avenue, from G. M. Hopkins, *City Atlas of Newport, Rhode Island* (Philadelphia, 1876). Newport Historical Society. Photography courtesy of the Preservation Society of Newport County.

Richard Morris Hunt's house is one of many cottages that would line the newly expanded Bellevue Avenue, which took the place of Jew Street in 1853. As the first American to attend the École des Beaux-Arts in Paris, the premier school of fine art and architecture in western Europe during the nineteenth century, Hunt changed the face of much of American architecture during the course of his career. His buildings in Newport, on both Bellevue Avenue and Ochre Point, range from wooden summer villas in the picturesque manner in the 1860s to palatial stone houses inspired by classical European models in the 1890s. His work literally formed the basis of both Newport's picturesque and gilded districts.

Fig. 134 *(opposite)*

Bellevue Avenue, from G. M. Hopkins, *City Atlas of Newport, Rhode Island* (Philadelphia, 1876). Newport Historical Society. Photograph courtesy of the Preservation Society of Newport County.

Redwood Library (1748) by Peter Harrison and the John N. A. Griswold House (1862) by Richard Morris Hunt rest side by side on the eastern (right) portion of Bellevue Avenue, another example of classical eighteenth-century style and picturesque nineteenth-century form existing in close proximity, creating the multilayered architectural fabric of Newport.

CATHERINE

Geo. A. Hazard
3714

David King
13418

Chas. P. Hazard
9315

David King
6844

Edwd Cunningham
12749

COTTAGE

Hop.

2840

Saml F. Hopkins hrs.

Elbert J. Anderson
14318

Wm. Andrews
4000

Apple
3088

Eliz. & Emma

ST.

Geo. C. Mason
75470

Mary C. Thibault
6373

Lucia R. W. Curtis
42543

Freh W. Rhinelander
9800

Frederick Tompkins
13136

Hamilton B. Tompkins
8505

REDWOOD ST.

Geo. H. Wilson
6700

Abbie D. Weaver
7343

Eliz. & Gage
11296

ST.

E. L. Brinle
14000

Margt
LaFarg

3

Charlotte Tompkins
15630

ALL SAINTS CHAPEL
10357

SUNNYSIDE

Jas. L. &
Hazar
14

BELLEVUE

REDWOOD

REDWOOD LIBRARY
37974

Wm. H. Ashhurst
53947

BEACH

2328

COTTAGE

Wm Edgar
87231

Ph.
S.

LIVERY STABLE
4841

Jno. West
5683

2280

2280

Tews

Lucius D. Davis
117300

PLACE

William Edgar

ICE HOUSE

Mar
& A

Jno. N. A. Griswold
84722

STATE

J. H. Hayward
4878

J. R. Gardiner
10032

Jas. Smith
4033

Jas. C. Clarke
2691

W. O. Greene
4203

COURT

PLACE

Thos. R. Gardiner
10009

Kath E. Wolf
3382

Job Tew
5631

DOWNING ST.

DOWNING BLOCK

George T. Downing
45036

CARRIAGE REPOSITORY

LIVERY

Peter & Geo. T. Downing
10007

Danl T. Swinburne Hrs.
14130

Jas. Clark

H. Hurry
1071/4

Perry Sherman
211049

Wm Edgar
33157

Danl T. Swinburne
86690

Mary Diggles
4166

GREEN HOUSE
16839

Saml Smith
2500

D. T. Swinburn, Hrs.

Wm. Sisson
4121

H. D. Deblois
4540

Benj. Bateman
4146

AVE.

Jno Malgen & Jno Malgen
3863

4060

8225

D. T. Swinburn Hrs.

DEBLOIS CT.

Harrigan LIVERY

D. T. Swinburne Hrs.
4730

Danl T. Swinburne

Jas W.

H. Hurry
4422

GREEN HOUSE

John Fadden
18239

Wm. S. Vose
17357

Thos.

Geo. Roblins

John Jackson
8836

Belinda Large

John
9153

Smith

Smith

Hazard
6025

Crandall
6331

T. W. & Charity Fisher
3060

12844

Luke Waters
8526

EDGAR

BATH

Fig. 135

The picturesque Pratt Cottage by Newport architect Dudley Newton, with men in a horse cart, ca. 1900, photograph. Newport Historical Society, P92.

The city created for summer colonists required scores of workers to keep cottages and villas to a polished perfection in season. In winter, depicted in the photograph, most of Bellevue Avenue's houses were boarded up, waiting for the social whirl of the next summer.

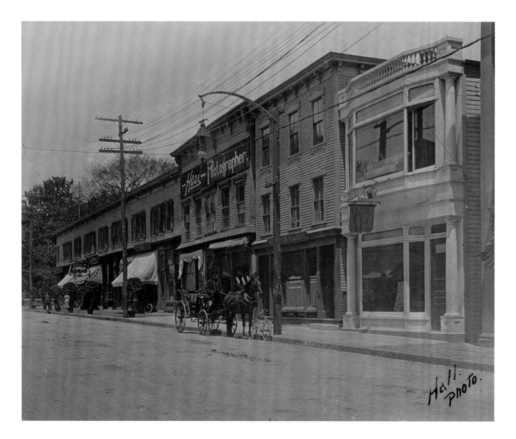

Fig. 136

The Downing Block, ca. 1890, photograph. Newport Historical Society, P753.

This commercial block on the northern sector of Bellevue Avenue was built by the African American businessman George Downing, a successful caterer, real estate developer, and civic benefactor.

Fig. 137 *(right)*

The Casino Block, from L. J. Richards and Co., *Atlas of the City of Newport* (Springfield, MA, 1907). Newport Historical Society.

Created in 1879–80 by the newly formed firm of McKim, Mead and White for James Gordon Bennett, the Newport Casino provided recreational activities, namely tennis, a theater, and shops for the burgeoning summer colony of fashion. This block of Bellevue Avenue also featured other major commercial buildings, including the Travers Block (1872) by Richard Morris Hunt.

Fig. 138 *(below)*

The Travers Block, ca. 1890, photograph. Clarence Stanhope Collection, Newport Historical Society, P739.

Designed in the Stick Style, featuring half-timbering inspired by French Medieval building, Richard Morris Hunt's Travers Block provided Bellevue Avenue with its first fashionable row of stores.

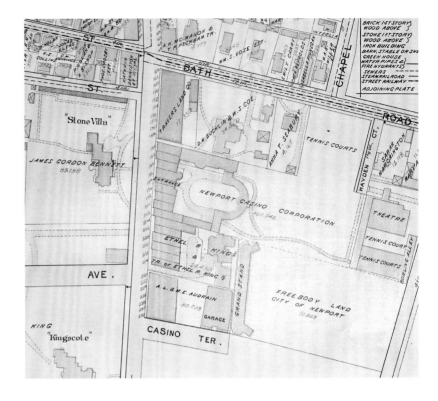

Ocean House   Bellevue Ave.   Burned September 1898

Fig. 139

The Ocean House Hotel, ca. 1880, photograph. Newport Historical Society, P2339.

Fig. 140

Walking on Bellevue Avenue with the Travers Block in the background, ca. 1890, photograph. Clarence Stanhope Collection, Newport Historical Society, P8661.

Fig. 141 *(right)*

Bellevue Avenue, ca. 1890, photograph. Clarence Stanhope Collection, Newport Historical Society, P740.

Fig. 142 *(below)*

Ochre Point, from L. J. Richards and Co., *Atlas of the City of Newport* (Springfield, MA, 1907). Newport Historical Society.

Ochre Point, once part of the Lawrence farm, evolved into an enclave of early Newport cottages. Ochre Court (1891), designed by Richard Morris Hunt for Ogden Goelet (upper portion of map), was the first of the palatial stone houses in Newport inspired by classical European models. The immense scale of the house and its entrance drive and forecourt planned on a straight axis introduced a monumentality and formality to Newport's urban landscape.

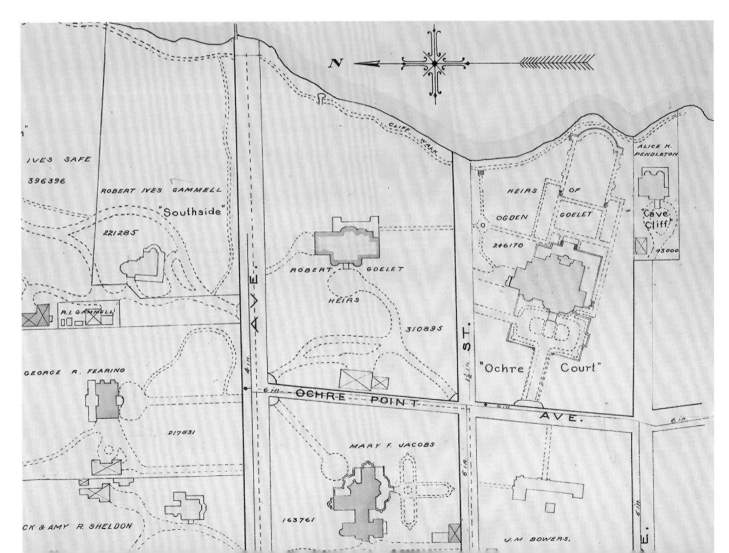

Fig. 143

Ochre Point Avenue, ca. 1890, photograph.
Gift of Lloyd A. Robinson, Newport Historical
Society, P8816.

A gabled summer villa rises above the clipped hedges
and trees of Ochre Point Avenue, laid out in 1877.
The desire for privacy in a summer resort designed
for both houses and people to see and be seen
resulted in a streetscape that partly revealed and, at
the same time, concealed its architectural treasures
and fashionable occupants.

Fig. 144 *(left)*

Newport's evolving streetscape, from G. M. Hopkins,
City Atlas of Newport, Rhode Island (Philadelphia,
1876). Newport Historical Society. Photograph
courtesy of the Preservation Society of Newport County.

Fig. 145 *(opposite)*

The Kay–Catherine–Old Beach Road district, from
L. J. Richards and Co., *Atlas of the City of Newport*
(Springfield, MA, 1907). Newport Historical Society.

The Kay–Catherine–Old Beach Road
area, in a northeast sector of Newport
bordered by Bellevue Avenue on the west
and Bath Road to the south (Fig. 145),
was one of the earliest instances of
land subdivision by the Gibbs family,
long established in the city since the
colonial period and owning large tracts
of property facing Easton's Pond. In
1845, the Gibbs Estate was organized
into lots for sale (Fig. 146), and by the
1870s, the family organized the Gibbs

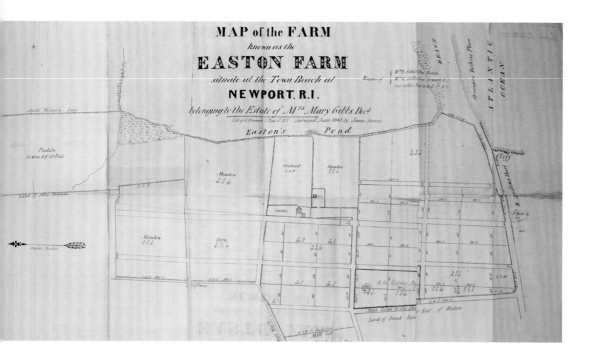

Fig. 146

The division of the Easton Farm by the Gibbs family, from G. Hayward, *Map of the Farm known as the Easton Farm …* (New York, 1845). Newport Historical Society.

The plan for the Easton Farm is one of the earliest examples of land subdivision as Newport transitioned from a site for agriculture toward commerce and real estate speculation. The map lists the use of land for corn, meadows, and orchards, while the remainder of the acreage is dedicated to parcels for sale as house lots.

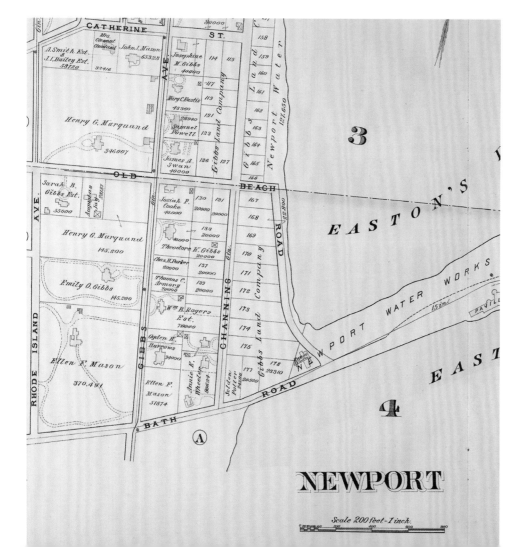

Fig. 147

Gibbs family land subdivision, from L. J. Richards and Co., *Atlas of the City of Newport* (Springfield, MA, 1893). Newport Historical Society. Photograph courtesy of the Preservation Society of Newport County.

The Gibbs family, with a lineage that traced back to Newport's colonial era, emerged in the nineteenth century as major landowners transforming their extensive farmlands into house lots. By the 1890s, they had formed the Gibbs Land Company to manage the growth of their real estate holdings.

Fig. 148

View of Ochre Point Avenue, ca. 1885, photograph. Clarence Stanhope Collection, Newport Historical Society, P9293.

The towered gate lodge at the main entrance to Vinland (1883), the summer residence of Catherine Lorillard Wolfe. Inspired by the legend of the Stone Tower in Touro Park as a creation of the Vikings, Miss Wolfe named her Ochre Point estate "Vinland," the supposed title given to Newport by the Vikings. The Boston firm of Peabody and Stearns designed the gate lodge, main house, and estate service buildings with rusticated stone facades adorned in Romanesque Revival–style ornament in what many dubbed the "Viking Revival" style. There is no conclusive evidence that Norse seafarers built any structures in Newport, but the myth of their foray in the area inspired one of its most romantic nineteenth-century summer houses.

Land Company (Fig. 147) as the potential for income grew with Newport's burgeoning reputation as a seaside resort.[45] In this age of entrepreneurial land development, by far one of the most successful figures was Alfred Smith, described by the *New York Times* as, "Newport's millionaire real estate agent, whose mortgages upon the property of prominent villa owners on all aristocratic thoroughfares runs up into the hundreds of thousands. … Mr. Smith did much for Newport, and not a few of the … thoroughfares so attractive to Newport visitors owe their existence to his energy …"[46]

The description of Newport's newer streets as "aristocratic" is indicative of a very focused and successful marketing strategy since real estate continued to rise in value as the city became ever-more fashionable with an emphasis on increasing social exclusivity. Hotels, such as the Atlantic House (1840) and Ocean House (1843) appeared on Bellevue Avenue, but the private villa would come

to define the new streets. The building boom in resort architecture on subdivided farmland moved at a quick pace, as reported by the noted poet and editor of *Picturesque America* (1872), William Cullen Bryant.

> *Cottages—everything here is called a cottage— every variety of architecture. Swiss, Gothic, French, Elizabethan, and American, and of every degree of cost, from the humbler structure that is rented for a thousand a year up to the stately mansion in which hundreds of thousands are invested, line the spacious avenues …* [47]

These early summer houses were originally set in windswept meadows, but, influenced by the prevailing taste for the picturesque, imported specimen trees made their entry on the scene by the 1880s. As the century progressed, Bellevue Avenue became a pageant of houses, gates, fences, and lush

REAR VIEW OF THE CASINO.

Fig. 149

C. Graham, "The Drive," *Harper's Weekly*, August 28, 1883, lithograph. Preservation Society of Newport County, PSNC.3637.

The pageant of horses and carriages before the Newport Casino on Bellevue Avenue, a daily ritual of the fashionable set.

greenery (Figs. 148 and 149), all a backdrop for the daily carriage rides where the eminent, the beautiful, the rich, and the powerful could see and be seen. Here, society could be on endless dress parade.

Newport had the distinction of being a resort of fashion, of the most current tastes complemented by the remnants of a venerable history, and it was the

Fig. 150

J. A. Williams, The Bruen Villa, ca. 1890, photograph. Newport Historical Society, P5765.1.

This shingled villa on Bellevue Avenue was designed circa 1880 by architect William Ralph Emerson.

Fig. 151

The Loring Andrews House, from George Champlin Mason, "Newport and Its Cottages," 1875. Newport Historical Society, P5770.

engine that drove the creation of the Bellevue Avenue district. The old colonial quarter slumbered in faded tones while the recently developed streets of summer villas beamed in the newest and brightest colors. Fashion, in its truest sense, never stands still. It is always moving forward in search of the next, most interesting, intriguing, or provocative expression. The houses of Bellevue Avenue and Ochre Point offered American architects a veritable laboratory for experimentation (Figs. 150 and 151). Every current style could be perfected and then duly recognized in lithographs and engravings by the Newport artist John Perry Newell. He capitalized on the construction boom by selling prints of the most recently completed houses. Many of Newport's latest villas also featured in publications by nationally renowned authors such as Andrew Jackson Downing, who showcased the

Edward King House (1845) in his best-selling book *The Architecture of Country Houses* (1850).[48]

Andrew Jackson Downing was one of the foremost advocates of landscape design and architecture in the picturesque manner—defined by serpentine drives, asymmetrical groupings of specimen plants and trees, and buildings that seamlessly integrated with their natural surroundings. As a nurseryman in the Hudson River Valley and, later, a prominent writer, he influenced a generation of landscape architects, notably Frederick Law Olmsted Sr. and Calvert Vaux, who devised comprehensive plans for introducing nature into the city in the form of tree-lined parkways and public parks. Downing's vision for America was a picturesque paradise of houses set on their own plots of land in architectural styles appropriate to the moral tone set by the owners. A learned man might have

157

Fig. 152

Roselawn, ca. 1860, photograph. Gift of Mr. Pierson Scott, Newport Historical Society, P9300.

The original farmhouse was remodeled as a Gothic Revival–style summer villa in the 1840s for James T. Rhodes. The age of agricultural pursuits was over by the mid-nineteenth century, replaced by the delights of the leisurely pastimes of summer visitors.

an Italianate villa, displaying his classical education. Another owner might have a Gothic Revival cottage, a symbol of Christian virtue.[49] With their towers, bay windows, and porches covered in vines and opening to landscapes set with winding paths, weeping trees, and flower beds, these houses sat in harmony with nature and offered a very romanticized, version of domestic paradise (Fig. 152). Llewellyn Park, New Jersey (1859), a planned community of serpentine roads with lots filled with houses of every picturesque variety, was one of the earliest expressions of Downing's utopian dream.[50] This became the model, spreading across the nation in planned towns from Brookline, Massachusetts, to Shaker Heights, Ohio. Unlike these communities, Bellevue Avenue and Ochre Point were not the result of one single stroke of planning by the hand of one designer, but the effect was the same. These districts evolved over decades, the result of real estate developers with eyes securely set on profit, promoters aware of both the aesthetic and monetary value of scenery, and architects who capitalized on the notoriety that building a Newport

cottage brought to one's career and reputation. While there were many motivations at work, the result was singular, an ensemble of houses set in spectacular natural environments that encapsulated the very values of the picturesque ideal in American urban planning.

In the romantic sensibilities that permeated nineteenth-century American culture, the myth of Newport emerged in the hands of painters, illustrators, photographers, and writers inspired by its now two-centuries-old past, drawn to its setting and fascinated by its architectural growth. They also came to reflect on the place and the social mores of its occupants. The interplay of past and present became a central theme in the work of many. They used Newport as their canvas not only for the color, light, and texture offered by its scenery and buildings, but for the foibles of human character displayed by its inhabitants. In 1873, Thomas Wentworth Higginson set his book *Oldport Days* in Newport, where old and new intersect and intermingle:

Each season brings its own attractions. In summer one may relish what is new in Oldport, as the liveries, the incomes, the manners. There is often a delicious freshness about these exhibitions; it is a pleasure to see some opulent citizen in his first kid gloves.

His newborn splendor stands in such brilliant relief against the "Old Stone Mill," the only thing on the Atlantic shore which has had time to forget its birthday! But in winter, the Old Mill gives the tone to the society around it; we then bethink ourselves of the crown upon our Trinity Church steeple, and resolve the courtesies of a bygone age shall linger here.[51]

Fig. 153

Engraving of the Stone Tower in Touro Park, *Harper's Weekly*, August 24, 1867. Newport Historical Society, 98.87.

The Stone Tower was one of Newport's earliest architectural mysteries and sightseeing attractions. Legend attributed it to the Vikings, a nineteenth-century theory not supported by twentieth-century archaeological research. Fiction proved far more alluring than fact as artists and writers throughout the centuries have celebrated the structure in paint, poetry, and prose as a witness to past times.

The Old Stone Mill mentioned by Higginson is the Stone Tower at Touro Park, one of the oldest and most monumental structures in Newport and one of its earliest sightseeing attractions (Fig. 153). During the early 1800s, a legend arose that the tower was built by Vikings. No archaeological evidence has emerged to support this story, but the myth was far more popular than the facts. Higginson conveniently used the mystique of the tower as a foil for the fashion-seeking parvenu, the old and new in Newport played against each other.

Fig. 154

View of Ocean Avenue, ca. 1890, photograph.
Newport Historical Society, P5640.

Designed to contour to the rolling hills and rocky
promontories of the southern coast of Newport,
Ocean Avenue is one of the earliest scenic drives in
the United States.

Newport's increasing social whirl in the post–Civil
War years required a broader stage and the city's
promoters and real estate developers were ready to
act. As Bellevue Avenue and the adjacent areas of
Ochre Point filled with houses, attention turned to the
southwestern portion of the island for new territory.
Not only did local Newporters speculate in land during
this period, but summer residents purchased extensive
acreage for investment in the present-day Ocean Drive

area.[52] George Champlin Mason had championed
the idea of a seaside drive along the rocky southern
coastline since the 1850s. With the success of Bellevue
Avenue, he knew that the natural scenery of the island
was its prime attraction, but remaining undeveloped
lands needed to be made accessible. His vision was a
road system along the southern and western coastline
of Newport. Once again, he used his role as editor of
the *Newport Mercury* to advance his cause:

> *on the subject of drives and walks we cannot*
> *ask better than to urge on all interested (and*
> *who are not?) the advantages to be derived*
> *from an open shore road around the whole*
> *southern portion of the Island … such a road*
> *is much wanted by all who love to stroll near*
> *the seashore, if opened it would immediately*
> *become a fashionable drive of an afternoon.*[53]

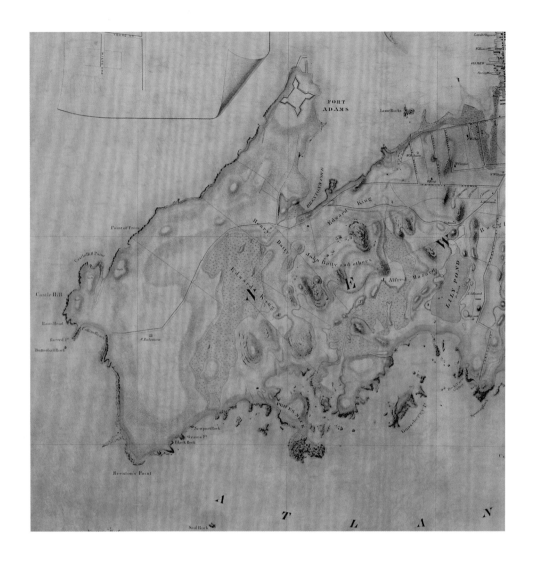

Fig. 155

Map of the Township of Newport and Middletown (detail of the south coast of Newport), from Sarony, Major and Knapp Lithographers, Coastal Survey Department, ca. 1860. Courtesy of Mr. & Mrs. S. Matthews V. Hamilton, Jr.

The open meadows and rocky promontories on the southern coast of Newport are evident in this map, created seven years before Ocean Avenue provided scenic vistas of the ocean, marshes, ponds, and hills of the district. The rugged topography of this region was in direct contrast to the flat terrain of Bellevue Avenue, the first site of nineteenth-century summer villas.

Edward King, John Alfred Hazard, Robert Kennedy, and Seth Bateman, all owners of large tracts of land throughout Newport, and specifically in the southwestern portion of the city, made Mason's dream become a reality (Fig. 154). In 1863, these gentlemen commissioned the Boston civil engineer S. L. Minot with detailed instructions as follows:

survey, stake out and plat said road not less than fifty feet in width, and execute a proper ... deed ... rights of way to the said city of

Newport ... for public travel from the westerly boundary of the land of Messrs. Bailey and Smith around to the beach at 'Castle Hill,' as near the sea shore as practicable ... the location to be left to S.L. Minot Civil Engineering under the direction of the respective owners.[54]

Completed in 1868, Ocean Avenue presented an entirely new approach to road layout and construction compared to the axial formality and manicured quality of Bellevue Avenue (Figs. 155 and 156). S. L. Minot's

Fig. 156

Ocean Avenue, from G. M. Hopkins, *City Atlas of Newport, Rhode Island* (Philadelphia, 1876). Newport Historical Society. Photograph courtesy of the Preservation Society of Newport County.

John Alfred Hazard was one of the primary speculators supporting the implementation of Ocean Avenue, which passed directly through his land.

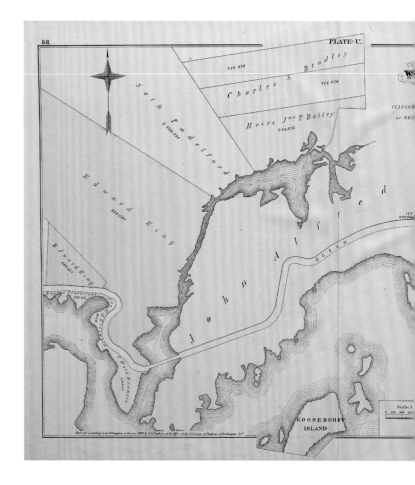

drive along the coastline ran throughout a rugged topography of hills, valleys, coves, and rocky promontories.[55] These picturesque features became an essential part of Ocean Avenue's design. At the same time Minot planned Ocean Avenue, Frederick Law Olmsted was completing the serpentine drives of Central Park in New York, establishing him as the acknowledged leader of landscape design in the United States and an expert at integrating nature and scenery into his roadways. Olmsted's entry into the evolution of Newport's streetscapes began in 1884, when the King, Glover, and Bradley families, who between them owned over three hundred acres of rolling hillside on the northern side of Ocean Drive (Fig. 157), commissioned Olmsted to plan a circuit of roads.[56] The informality of the scheme and the respect for the natural topography of the region distinguish Olmsted's creation, who described his work in an 1885 report:

> nearly three miles of roads shown are already built and the remaining part ... agreed to be built. They follow natural passes, admitting of easy trotting grades. Their wheelways are broader and better graded than that of the well-known Ocean Avenue, their draining more thorough and their metaling deeper and firmer. As may be seen by the key-map, they form parts of continuous circuits for pleasure driving in connection with Bellevue, Harrison and Ocean Avenues and establish conveniently direct communication between all parts of the district and the town, beach, harbor and other points of interest.[57]

Olmsted completed the transformation of the southwestern portion of Newport from windswept hills to subdivided house lots linked with a comprehensive road system that appealed to sightseers. This development enabled the expansion of the summer resort from the easterly Kay–Catherine–Old Beach Road district, Bellevue Avenue, and Ochre Point to the southern and western

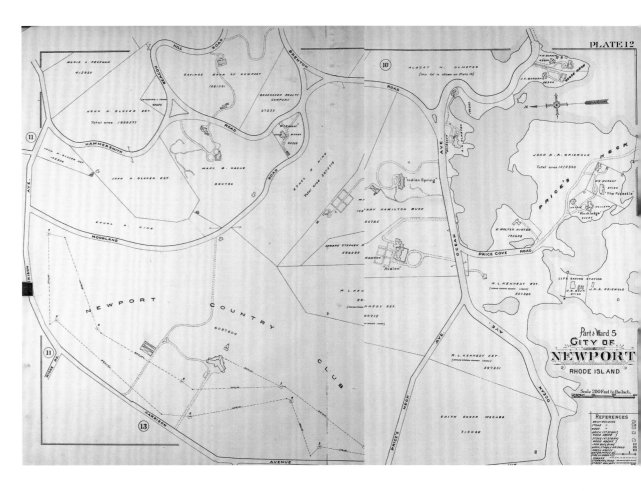

coastlines of the city. Critics approved, among them Mariana Griswold Van Rensselaer, who stated in *Garden and Forest*, "The new roads are admirably disposed for convenience and beauty."[58] These last two words, written by one of the most renowned architecture and landscape writers of the era, distilled the motivations and aspirations of the whole cadre of characters who developed Newport as a summer resort in the age of the picturesque. By the 1890s, however, a new aesthetic emerged reflecting a new social tenor. Monumentality and a gilded classical grandeur would be the driving forces in both architecture and the social mores it exhibited, making their impressions upon the Queen of Resorts.

Fig. 157

A plan of Ocean Avenue and Price's Neck, from L. J. Richards and Co., *Atlas of the City of Newport* (Springfield, MA, 1907). Newport Historical Society.

Hammersmith, Beacon Hill, and Moorland Farm Roads encompass the extensive network of roads planned by Frederick Law Olmsted Jr. from 1884 to 1885 as part of the King, Glover, and Bradley families' combined lands as a district of picturesque houses. This was the last major urban road system added to Newport until the creation of America's Cup Avenue in the mid-1960s.

The curving roads follow the natural topography of rocky coves and steep hills, the dramatic setting for two houses: the Busk residence (1889) by Richard Morris Hunt and "Wildacre" (1901) by California architect Irving Gill for Albert Charles Olmsted, the half brother of famed landscape designer Frederick Law Olmsted Jr.

163

THE GILDED CITY
1890–1914

Hadn't it been above all, in good faith, the Age of Beauties—the blessed age when it was so easy to be a Beauty on the Avenue.

Henry James, "The Sense of Newport," *Harper's Monthly Magazine*, August 1906

DURING THE 1890S, SOCIETY BEAUTIES; DEVOTEES of sailing, tennis, and polo; and some of the nation's captains of industry and finance imposed a gilded realm of imperial opulence and architectural monumentality upon the picturesque wooden villas of Bellevue Avenue and Ochre Pont. Richard Morris Hunt led the way. As the first American architect to be trained at the École des Beaux-Arts in Paris, he had seen firsthand the historic châteaux and palaces of Europe, which he would recreate on the cliffs of Newport. He mastered the principles of classical design, from rationally developed planning to the precise rendering of historically inspired detail. Furthermore, he understood how to create architectural pageantry as a setting for social theater.

In 1897, *Munsey's Magazine* reported, "Society in Newport is always on dress parade …"[59] The afternoon carriage ride on Bellevue Avenue became a key moment in this social ritual, a time when this wide thoroughfare, lined with imposing gates and houses maintained with polished perfection, played as a backdrop to fashion (Fig. 158). Consuelo Vanderbilt Balsan recalled, "we proceeded in state down Bellevue Avenue. And society rolled by in the elegant equipages one saw in those days when to be well turned out

Fig. 158

Main gates of Beechwood, ca. 1890, photograph. Newport Historical Society, P1136.

The Bellevue Avenue estate of Mr. and Mrs. William Backhouse Astor, the acknowledged leader of Newport's social summer colony, provided only a glimpse of the house beyond the elaborate iron gates.

on wheels with a handsome pair of horses was as necessary to one's standard of luxury as a fine house."[60]

The Beaux-Arts classicism espoused by Hunt and his contemporaries, aided by the riches of America's business oligarchs, produced an enclave of palatial houses in Newport that bespoke a new aristocracy of wealth (Fig. 159). Buildings of Herculean scale and a European-inspired splendor began to appear throughout the nation in the 1890s, the decade when the United States surpassed Great Britain, France, and Germany in the production of coal, steel, and oil. Now a world economic force, the financial titans and self-proclaimed social arbiters of the United States endowed their home cities and summer resorts with architectural extravagances to express this newfound supremacy. In *American Estates and Gardens*, Barr Ferree listed in detail grand residences across the country. His chapter entitled, "A Group of Newport Palaces," highlighted the idea behind the conspicuous display:

The architectural thought that lay behind the creation of Versailles is identical with the ideas that have brought the great houses of Newport into existence. It is true that Versailles was a single palace, built by a despotic monarch for his own delight, while Newport is an aggregation of palaces, built not by despots, but by free American citizens. But the palace of Versailles was a vast architectural background for court fetes and festivities of all sorts. Just so the palaces of Newport are architectural backgrounds for the pleasures and sports of its inhabitants ... Newport, at all events, illustrates

Fig. 159

Newport Houses, ca. 1910, postcard. Newport Historical Society, P4169.

The architectural variety and material splendor of Newport's Gilded Age summer houses were the subject of public fascination. These buildings often featured in magazines and on postcards. Bellevue Avenue, Ochre Point, and Ocean Drive offered up a pageant of historic revival-style architecture.

splendid living in the most splendid fashion it has yet attained in America, so far as a group of houses and people is concerned.[61]

Ferree's celebratory and overtly nationalistic language articulates the historical inspirations and cultural aspirations evident in the houses that transformed the streetscapes of Bellevue Avenue and Ochre Point. The new stone and marble palaces were most assertively a courtly setting for a power elite who transformed the picturesque wooden seaside resort of the mid-nineteenth century into a gilded spectacle at the dawn of the twentieth century.

Privacy, distance, and exclusion were made manifest by high gates and iron fences that closed off the recently built French châteaux and Italian

Fig. 160

View of The Breakers, ca. 1900, photograph.
Newport Historical Society, P9454.

The gates and fence of The Breakers (1893–5) for
Cornelius Vanderbilt by Richard Morris Hunt.
The original wooden Queen Anne Revival–style
house known as The Breakers, (1877) burned to the
ground in 1892, prompting the building of a new
house. The stage was set for monumental change.
Hunt created a villa in the Italian Renaissance style
and replaced the earlier low cast-iron fence with a
high wall and opulent stone gates, radically altering
the character of Ochre Point. The picturesque villas
of the district with their low walls allowed for
uninterrupted views across the area. In the 1890s,
classically inspired houses, such as The Breakers,
included high walls for privacy.

palazzi. Baroque and neoclassical-style pillars, posts,
and elaborate metalwork marked the streetscapes of
Bellevue Avenue and Ochre Point (Fig. 160). Rather
than the curving drives, serpentine walks, and low
cast-iron fences of mid-nineteenth-century Gothic
Revival, Italianate, and Queen Anne Revival villas,
the Beaux-Arts palaces were triumphantly framed by
entrance courts and drives in formal, straight axes, all
focused on the exhibition of power and pomp through
reference to history and fantasy (Figs. 161–68).

Grandiose houses as fixtures in Newport's urban
scenography elicited both praise and censure from
architectural critics and social commentators alike.
Henry James wrote a prescient observation of both
the built and natural environment when he visited
in 1906. His poignant recollections cast the streets,
buildings, and topography as places of memory:

> thanks to the pilers-on of gold ... it now
> bristles with the villas and palaces into which
> the cottages have now turned ... it was most
> touching of all to go back to dimmest days,

> such as now appear anti-deluvian, when
> ocean-drives, engineered by landscape artists
> and literally macadamized all the way, were
> still in the lap of time.[62]

The myth of a lost paradise permeates James's writing.
He used the city in its entirety, both its natural and
human-made features, as a metaphor for the state of
American culture. As he wandered the old town and
the newer districts, he abandoned longings for the
past and turned instead to criticism of the present and
forebodings for the future, releasing the full weight of
his prophetic powers on the gilded realms of Bellevue
Avenue and Ochre Point.

> The white elephants, as one may call them,
> all cry and no wool, all house and no garden,
> make now, for three or four miles, a barely
> interrupted chain, and I dare say I think of them
> best, and of the distressful, inevitable waste they
> represent. The place itself was more than ever,
> to the fancy, like some dim simplified ghost of

Fig. 161 *(left)*

Map of the Township of Newport and Middletown (detail of Ochre Point), from Sarony, Major and Knapp Lithographers, Coastal Survey Department, ca. 1860. Courtesy of Mr. & Mrs. S. Matthews V. Hamilton, Jr.

Ochre Point in 1860 was occupied primarily by the Lawrence farm. Land was purchased by various owners, but not immediately built upon. In the ensuing decade, this point of land became an enclave of grand summer houses designed by the nation's leading architects.

Fig. 162 *(right)*

Ochre Point, from G. M. Hopkins, *City Atlas of Newport, Rhode Island* (Philadelphia, 1876). Newport Historical Society. Photograph courtesy of the Preservation Society of Newport County.

In 1876, Ochre Point was still largely rural. When Ochre Point Avenue was created in 1877, Pierre Lorillard built The Breakers on the site of the Lawrence farm, the final transformation of the area from agricultural to residential.

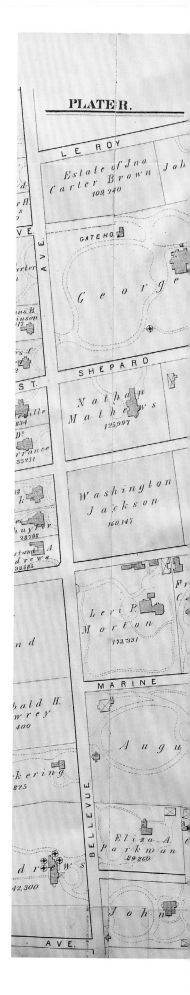

a small Greek island where the clear walls of some pillared portico or pavilion, perched afar, looked like those temples of the gods, and where Nature, deprive of that ease in merely massing herself on which 'American Scenery,' as we lump it together, to apt to depend for its effect, might have shown a piping shepherd on a hillside or attached a mythic image to any point of rocks. What an idea, originally, to have seen this miniature spot of earth, where the sea-nymphs of the curved sands, at worst, might have chanted back to the shepherds, a mere breeding-ground for white elephants![63]

The place James so loved and the monumental buildings he so despised became a touchstone for many on the debate about the meaning of art,

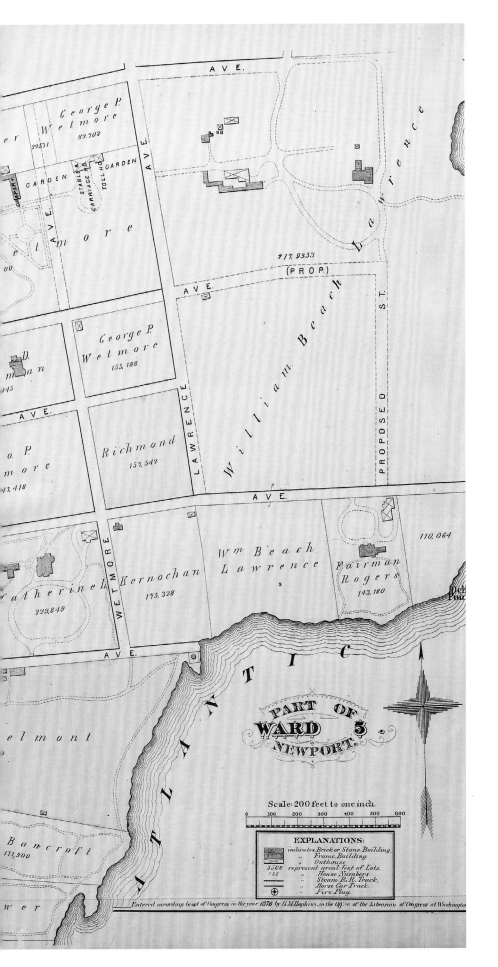

Fig. 163 *(below)*

The Breakers on Ochre Point, from L. J. Richards and Co., *Atlas of the City of Newport* (Springfield, MA, 1907). Newport Historical Society.

The redesign (1893–95) of The Breakers for Cornelius Vanderbilt introduced a classical formality to the urban scenery of Ochre Point. The straight drives and rectangular forecourt dominated views of the house from the street.

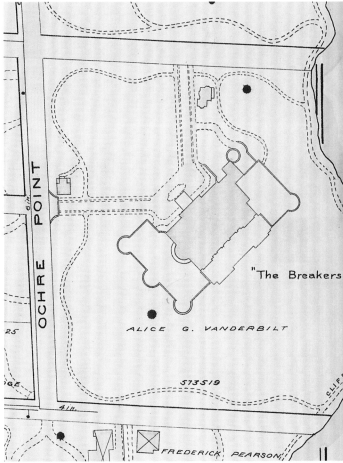

NEWPORT: THE ARTFUL CITY

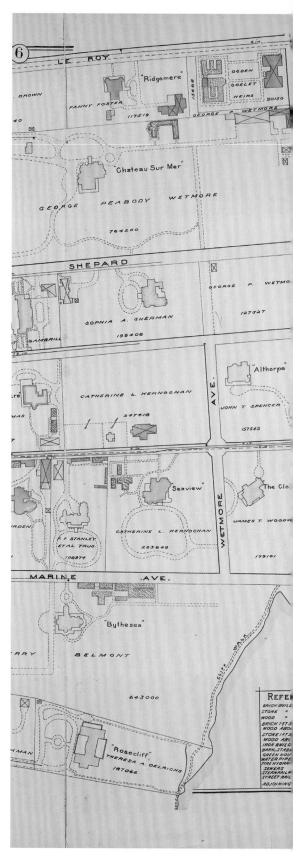

Fig. 164 *(above)*

View of southern portion of the Bellevue Avenue district, ca. 1920. Newport Historical Society, P8568.

The evolution of the summer resort is evident in this photograph of three houses. The Train Villa (right) is an early Victorian house; Inchiquin (center) is a late nineteenth-century Renaissance Revival–style villa; and Beech-Mound is in the Classical Revival style, its columned temple front reminiscent of Henry James's observations in "The American Scene" about the island appearing like some dim pillared ghost of a Greek island.

Fig. 165 *(right)*

Ochre Point, from L. J. Richards and Co., *Atlas of the City of Newport* (Springfield, MA, 1907). Newport Historical Society.

The entire area of Ochre Point was fully developed with summer estates by the early 1900s.

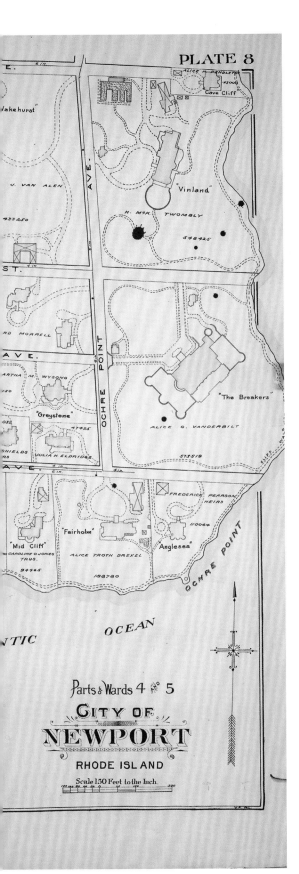

Fig. 166 *(above)*

Charles H. Seddon. Ochre Court, ca. 1910, postcard. Newport Historical Society, 2014.013.014.

The main gates and drive to Ochre Court (1891). Richard Morris Hunt's design for the entrance of Ochre Court established an entirely new template for the relationship of house to street in Newport summer villa architecture. A classical city of straight lines imposed itself on the curving outlines of the picturesque city that had dominated the Bellevue Avenue and Ochre Point districts from the 1840s through the 1880s.

Fig. 167 *(below)*

Views of The Breakers, ca. 1900, photograph. Newport Historical Society, P9458.

The grand scale of the perimeter garden wall, entrance gates, and the house itself defined the monumentality of Gilded Age Newport.

Fig. 168 *(opposite)*

Detail of Bellevue Avenue and Ocean Drive, from Galt and Hoy, *Newport, RI* (New York, 1878). Library of Congress, G3774.N4A3 1878 .G3.

This map represents the Newport Henry James longed for in his writings about the city, a time before the grand Beaux-Arts-inspired palaces appeared in the 1890s.

Fig. 169 *(above)*

Marble House, ca. 1900, photograph. Newport Historical Society, P2322.

Designed by Richard Morris Hunt for William Kissam and Alva Vanderbilt, Marble House (1888–92), on Bellevue Avenue, introduced a standard of opulence never before seen in Newport.

culture, and society as the nation basked in the high noon of an American Renaissance (Fig. 169). Newport's natural setting and artistic heritage prompted nostalgia for an imagined past while the luxurious excesses of the city's gilded mansions sparked virulent reaction. James's view of the future, however, could be as subjective as his remembrances of the past, open to equally romantic yearnings and hopes. Fearless in his judgment, James boldly decreed the fate of palatial houses and the grandiose skyline they imposed on the urban scene.

NEWPORT: THE ARTFUL CITY

They are queer and conscious and lumpish—some of them, as with an air of the brandished proboscis, really grotesque—which their averted owners roused from a witless dream wonder what in the world is to be done with them. The answer to which, I think, can only be that there is nothing to be done, nothing but to let them stand there always, vast and blank for reminder to those concerned of the witlessness, and peculiarly awkward vengeances of affronted proportion and discretion.[64]

James crafted an insightful portrait interweaving historical and emotional memory, keen observation, and contemporary criticism as he predicted doom for the gilded districts of the city (Fig. 170). Other artists approached Newport in their own way and with different skill sets. In each case, the city inspired and motivated them to address its mythic past, glamorous present, and uncertain future. In 1912, F. Lauriston Bullard, the Pulitzer Prize–winning editorial writer for the *Boston Herald*, extolled the virtues of the colonial quarter and doubted the value of the gilded city as he wrote,

nowhere else in America do romance, beauty and fashion so combine and ... charm the imaginative visitor by their odd mixing of old and new, and by the stories which history and tradition associate with the wharves and streets and quaint doorways ... to many the chief charm of Newport will be the realization of the romantic and historic as actual living presences,

pervading the whole place, brooding over the glittering present for the old houses, looking on calmly and undisturbed at all that wealth has wrought of luxury and display.[65]

Wealth and a taste for monumental scale, however analyzed and criticized, did not end with Bellevue Avenue. The vision many summer colonists had for their version of the perfect city came under threat, in the view of some, in 1889, when the electric street railway service made its way to Newport. Concerned about the impact of mass transportation on their prized community, a group of powerful summer residents formed a group with William Waldorf Astor as chairman, August Belmont as president, and Cornelius Vanderbilt as treasurer. The *Providence Journal* reported, "The Summer People Met to Declare War," and in a letter to Rhode Island Senator Nelson W. Aldrich, Astor stated, "such a road would be a standing danger to life, a serious detriment to the value of property, and an irreparable injury to the renowned beauty of the place."[66] Electric railway service did indeed begin in Newport in August 1889, entering the city via Broadway and running down Spring Street to Morton Park, and traversing Levin Street and Bath Road to access Easton's Beach. There were no streetcar tracks laid on Bellevue Avenue or Ocean Drive. The age of mass transportation had arrived, affecting the work and leisure habits of an increasing number of people. Newport as a summer resort, known for its exclusivity, would become less and less private with increased access via streetcars. A writer took a rather satirical view of these developments, reporting, "It is

DR. BARTON JACOBS RESIDENCE, NEWPORT, R. I.

Fig. 170

Dr. Henry Barton Jacobs House, "Whiteholme" at Narragansett and Ochre Point Avenues, 1925, photograph. Townsend Studios, Newport Historical Society, 2012.1.5.

The Classic Revival–style house by architect John Russell Pope is framed from the street by two grand posts with an axial drive focused on the main building.

Fig. 171

A lone streetcar traverses Bath Road, the main artery connecting Newport to Easton's Beach, ca. 1910, photograph. Newport Historical Society, P8614.

Newport's urban geography is characterized by its proximity to the sea with views of natural scenery at every turn. Established in 1889, electric street railway cars were part of an integrated transportation system linking Newport with nearby Middletown and Portsmouth, Rhode Island, and continuing on with a ferry connection to Bristol, Rhode Island, and railroad bridge to Fall River, Massachusetts.

Fig. 172

Electric street railway car on Bath Road, ca. 1890, photograph. Clarence Stanhope Collection, Newport Historical Society, P56.

the business of the city to take care of summer people … they objected to the progress of the 19th century here although they liked it at home."[67] He saw the irony in the captains of modern industry, with fortunes based in large part on technological advances, refusing to allow many of these features in their summer paradise. The protests of many residents did, however, have one positive impact: the formation in 1912 of the Newport Improvement Association (Fig. 173), which advocated for addressing the city's needs in ways that included the historic, the modern, and the natural.

In the early 1900s, a public-spirited vision came to the fore with Senator George Peabody Wetmore, a resident of Newport and a former governor of Rhode Island, who proposed an idea for a suitably impressive entrance to the city. His focus was on Bath Road, which led from Bellevue Avenue to Easton's Beach, replete with an electric street railway (Figs. 171 and 172). The narrow thoroughfare, in the senator's opinion, did not do justice to the beauty of the site. He committed himself to this project, writing, "It will give great pleasure to do anything in my power to bring about the widening that will be of such benefit to the community."[68] Senator Wetmore's interest in this cause was influenced by the redesign of Bath Road proposed in the 1913 improvement plan for Newport by the Olmsted Brothers for the Newport Improvement Association. Between 1915 and 1918,

the Olmsteds were also engaged on enhancement to the south entrance and service drives of Wetmore's Newport estate, Chateau-sur-Mer. Senator Wetmore served on the Commission of Fine Arts in Washington, DC, which at the time was undertaking major improvements to the National Mall, a project also involving the Olmsteds.[69] Victorian picturesque plantings and Gothic Revival–style buildings had been imposed on its original classical plan of broad, radiating avenues and formal green spaces. Work on

the Mall during the early 1900s was central to the City Beautiful movement, which advocated reform in both architecture and urban planning with the objective of introducing the classical grandeur of European cityscapes and parks to the United States. In this spirit, Senator Wetmore wrote of his hope for Bath Road as "a boulevard of great public usefulness and beauty."[70] Such sentiments combined the ideals of the City Beautiful movement and his own experiences in Washington. Senator Wetmore did not live to see the redesign of Bath Road, nor was the Olmsted scheme for its expansion into a parkway initially realized, but they were a portent of things to come. Construction on the road began in 1917 and, after periods of inactivity due to lack of funds, was completed in 1933 with the creation of two avenues divided by double rows of trees.[71] Senator Wetmore's political and social influence with property owners on the northern side of Bath Road resulted in their agreement to relinquish footage for expansion.

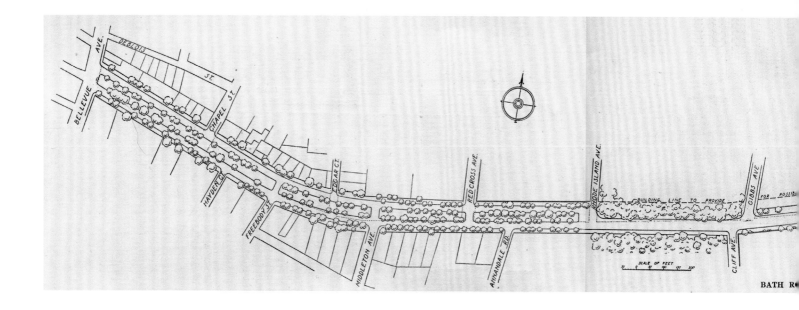

BATH R

In 1946, Bath Road was renamed Memorial Boulevard in honor of the men and women who served in World War II.[72]

Senator Wetmore achieved some of his objectives for a beautiful and dignified boulevard as an entry to Newport. Such lofty visions were few as the twentieth century presented the challenges of two world wars and economic depression, eradicating most of the social and financial conditions that spurred the creation of Newport's Gilded Age district. An atmosphere of faded beauty and physical decay pervaded the city, precisely noted in the 1944 article, "Life Visits a Fading Newport":

> *they stand in stately rows along Bellevue Avenue in Newport, RI, once 'the richest street in the world.' Since the passing of the Gilded Age that these houses symbolize, two wars, a long depression, high income taxes and a shortage of servants have dimmed Newport's splendor. The doors of these villas will never be opened again.*[73]

Life magazine appeared to justify Henry James's 1906 prediction that the great houses, the "white elephants," would someday stand vast and blank.

A new social order and modernist aesthetics had arrived in full force upon the scene. Financially, historic buildings were largely seen as economic burdens. Culturally, the historical revival styles and ornamental details of old buildings were viewed as relics of a corrupt past representing a slavish admiration for social hierarchy and the privilege of the few. Modernity, with its emphasis on efficiency and minimalism, had no time for the picturesque charms so often celebrated in earlier decades.

The historic houses of Bellevue Avenue were forced to face an uncertain fate beginning in 1957 when Stone Villa (ca. 1850) was demolished for the construction of a modernist shopping center. The villa's large landscape and mature trees, which once formed a partial canopy over Bellevue Avenue, were lost to the cityscape, replaced by a large parking lot. The Travers Block (1872), the Newport Casino (1880), the King Block (ca. 1890), and the Audrain Building (1901), directly across the avenue, were substantially impacted by this radical change in the scale of the district. The intimate quality of a tree-laden thoroughfare was lost. In the same year, on the next block to the south, another shopping center appeared on the open lot once occupied by the Atlantic House Hotel (burned to the ground in 1898).

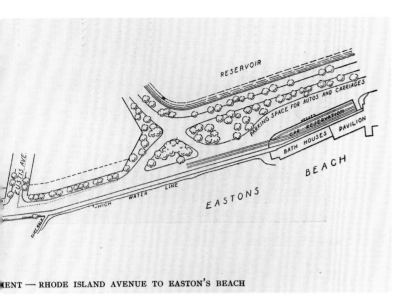

ENT — RHODE ISLAND AVENUE TO EASTON'S BEACH

Fig. 173

Analysis of primary roads in Newport, from Frederick Law Olmsted Jr., *Proposed Improvements for Newport*, 1913. Newport Historical Society.

Olmsted proposed the widening of Bath Road to a wide boulevard lined with trees.

The next major threat to Newport's Gilded Age landmarks came forth with a vengeance in 1962 when The Elms (1901), built by the Pennsylvania coal magnate Edward Julius Berwind, went on the auction block. Purchased by a developer, the estate faced demolition to make way for possible commercial development in the heart of the residential Bellevue Avenue corridor. Preservationists and private citizens, alarmed at the situation, organized to save The Elms. Cleveland Amory wrote "The Crucial Battle for Modern Newport" in the *New York Times Magazine* at the height of the controversy, stating, "Newport's Armageddon, in other words, had come. Whichever way The Elms blew, Newport was to follow."[74] Bulldozers and wrecking balls did not destroy The Elms, its thirteen acres of grounds, or its magnificent eighteenth-century, French-style stone and cast-iron fence lining Bellevue Avenue. The Preservation Society of Newport County, formed in 1945 to save the city's architectural and cultural heritage, acquired the estate in 1962 and opened it as a house museum, beginning a trend toward protecting endangered nineteenth- and early twentieth-century properties of architectural significance.

The picturesque and gilded districts created in the former meadows and seaside cliffs of Newport can be viewed as wholly unsustainable urban environments. Created in an age of wealth unfettered by income tax and requiring large staffs to maintain, the grand estates did not adhere to any of the principles of efficiency and cost-effectiveness of the mid-twentieth century or the century to come. Remarkably, these sites have not only survived, but have flourished. The predictions made by Henry James were, in fact, both prophetic and flawed. The great houses, and their attendant streets, could not function as they once did during the Gilded Age. Through a combination of historic preservation, heritage tourism, educational use, and private ownership, the essential character of Bellevue Avenue, Ochre Point, and Ocean Drive has been maintained against all odds. Such is the story of cities when inhabitants are committed to their survival through reinvention. The vagaries of time will tell if this very grand and majestic district will prevail. Cities rise and fall. It is the stuff of history. For the present, at least, one may still drive down the leafy boulevards and windswept seaside roads of Newport, past its wooden villas and marble palaces, and be reminded of historical ages both picturesque and gilded.

BROADWAY NORTH FROM BULL ST.

CHAPTER 4

VICTORIAN EXPANSION AND MODERN REINVENTION

Broadway and Points North

MEADOWLANDS AND CULTIVATED FIELDS overlooking Narragansett Bay, a vibrant Victorian era retail and residential area, and a site of both unrestrained twentieth-century development and community-driven preservation protest make the northern sector of Newport a story of expansion, decline, and revival. Unlike Washington Square and the Point, this area did not have artists and mythmakers aplenty to craft and celebrate the image of a heroic colonial past. It did not have the opulent social whirl and gilded houses of Bellevue Avenue and Ocean Drive. This northern district of Newport, however, has its preserved streets and buildings attesting to a booming, technologically advanced city that rose and, for the most part, fell during the course of the nineteenth century. And it was saved by its residents, who charted a course for the future.

Originally listed as "Broad Street" in the Blaskowitz map of 1777 (Fig. 174), Broadway was

There is a large number of mechanics here ... at least 2,000, most of these boarding, but many are desirous of going to housekeeping but find it impossible to procure tenements.

Newport Mercury, May 18, 1872

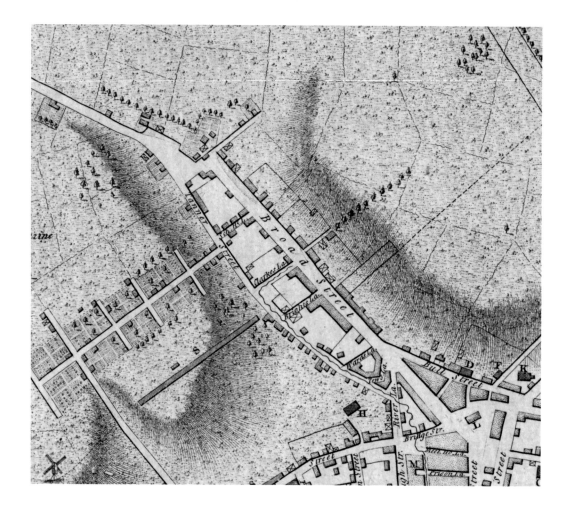

Previous spread

Broadway, ca. 1900,
photograph. Newport
Historical Society, P9280.

Fig. 174 *(left)*

Charles Blaskowitz, *Plan
of the Towne of Newport*
(detail of Broad Street), 1777.
Library of Congress.

the primary route leading out of town. It followed the path of least resistance on a level grade of land between two slopes. The thoroughfare began at the northeastern corner of the Parade, later Washington Square, and continued through fields and orchards to the northern boundary of Newport at One Mile Corner. Some of the earliest surviving colonial buildings, such as the Wanton-Lyman-Hazard House (1700), mark the first block of old Broad Street (Figs. 175–77), while tanneries, dyehouses, and ropewalks lined nearby Tanner Street, which originally gave way to farms, orchards, and large country estates. Throughout the colonial era, urban development focused on the Parade and the waterfront districts of the Point, the wharves of Thames Street, and Historic Hill. Agricultural production dominated the life of most of Broad Street until the mid-1800s, when advances in technology prompted a building boom along the renamed Broadway (Figs. 178 and 179).

The establishment of the Newport Water Works and the Newport Gas Company prompted the expansion of the city in the latter half of the nineteenth century. These were essential elements in the making of a modern, functioning, healthy city in accordance with nineteenth-century standards of urban planning.

They responded to advances in understanding the need for public utilities to prevent the outbreak of disease and provide greater comfort and convenience in daily life. Industrial technology also had a direct impact on land subdivision, street layout, and building construction. The steam-powered saw revolutionized the mass production of lumber and assembly-line methods made nails and other construction supplies available at affordable prices. The result was a general uniformity of land allotments and house dimensions. This movement toward standardization in the industrial age is clearly reflected in the areas to the east and west of Broadway (Figs. 180–83),

Fig. 177

Lower Broadway, ca. 1910, photograph. Newport Historical Society, P2473.

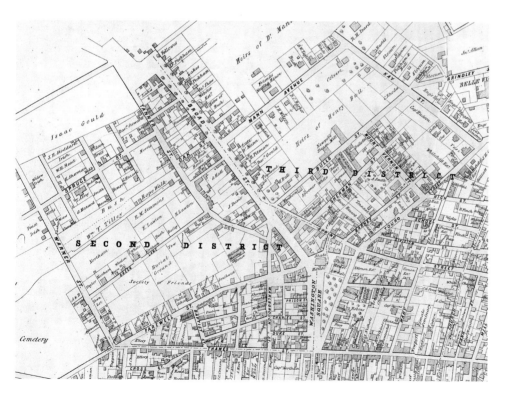

Fig. 178

Broadway, ca. 1850, from Matthew Dripps and B.I. Tilley, *Map of the City of Newport* (New York and Newport, RI, 1859). Newport Historical Society.

In the 1850s, real estate on both sides of Broadway was subject to increasing development. The open meadows of the colonial era were divided into lots for residential and commercial use.

Fig. 179

Map of the Township of Newport and Middletown (detail of Broadway), from Sarony, Major and Knapp Lithographers, Coastal Survey Department, ca. 1860. Courtesy of Mr. & Mrs. S. Matthews V. Hamilton, Jr.

This detail shows Broad Street, later renamed Broadway, the central artery leading from the heart of the city to open countryside. The topography of hills determined its placement as the most convenient route out of Newport. Tanner Street, to the left of Broad Street, was laid out along a stream, providing a freshwater source for the tanneries that gave the thoroughfare its name.

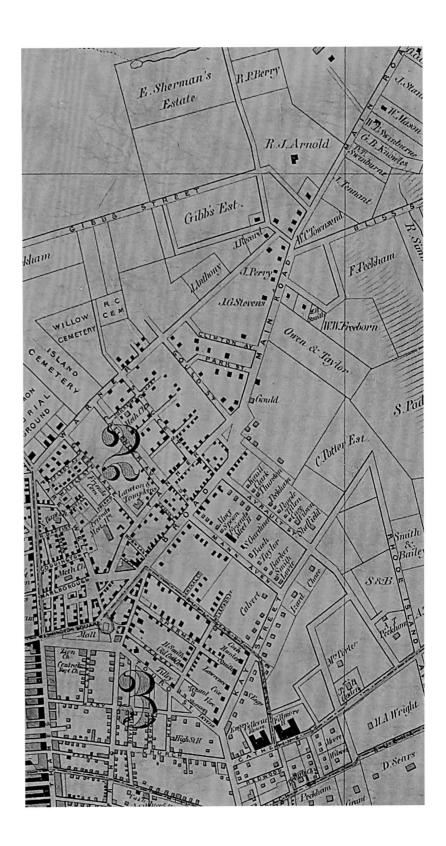

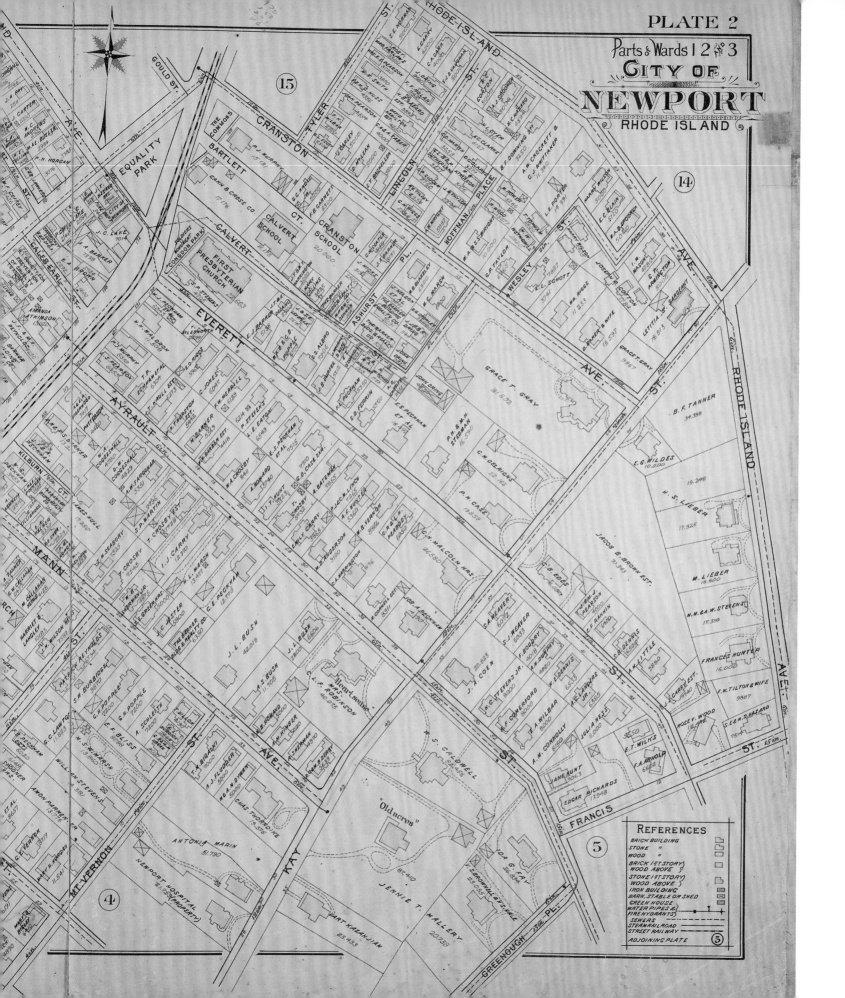

PLATE 2
Parts & Wards 1 2 & 3
CITY OF
NEWPORT
RHODE ISLAND

REFERENCES

Fig. 180 *(opposite)*

Land subdivisions along Broadway, from L. J. Richards and Co., *Atlas of the City of Newport* (Springfield, MA, 1907). Newport Historical Society.

Lands laid out in uniform house lots, the result of the standardization of real estate and building technology during the late 1800s and early 1900s.

Fig. 181 *(right)*

Streetcars in Newport (detail), from L. J. Richards and Co., *Atlas of the City of Newport* (Springfield, MA, 1907). Newport Historical Society.

The broken black line on Broadway indicates the route of electric street railways, which prompted the expansion of Newport along the east and west sides of Broadway.

which were developed from the 1860s through the early 1900s. The district had a high degree of mechanics and skilled laborers in many trades, as well as professionals in medicine and businesses related to shipping and commerce. Dry goods and hardware stores, pharmacies, bakeries, and furniture emporiums were among the many retail enterprises serving the needs of local residents. Newport Hospital, City Hall (Figs. 184–86), and several schools emerged as the thoroughfare's main landmarks, all of them key civic features of the Victorian cityscape.[75] In 1889, electric streetcars entered Newport by way of Broadway, which housed the major car shed for the line. Upon reaching lower Broadway, streetcars branched off in two directions: to Spring Street with the final destinations of Easton's Beach and Morton Park; and through Washington Square to Long Wharf. By 1920, the streetcar system extended well beyond the confines

Fig. 182 *(following page)*

Map of Broadway, from L. J. Richards and Co., *Atlas of the City of Newport* (Springfield, MA, 1907). Newport Historical Society.

The technology of the Industrial Revolution encroached on the pastoral landscape of the late eighteenth and early nineteenth centuries in the northern boundary of Broadway and West Main Road. The Old Colony Railroad located its main storage shed in this vicinity. The Greek Revival Elmhyrst (1835), once the center of a large country estate, appears reduced in acreage as the area near Hoppin Street was parceled into small house lots for workers who had access to the streetcar system introduced to Newport in 1889.

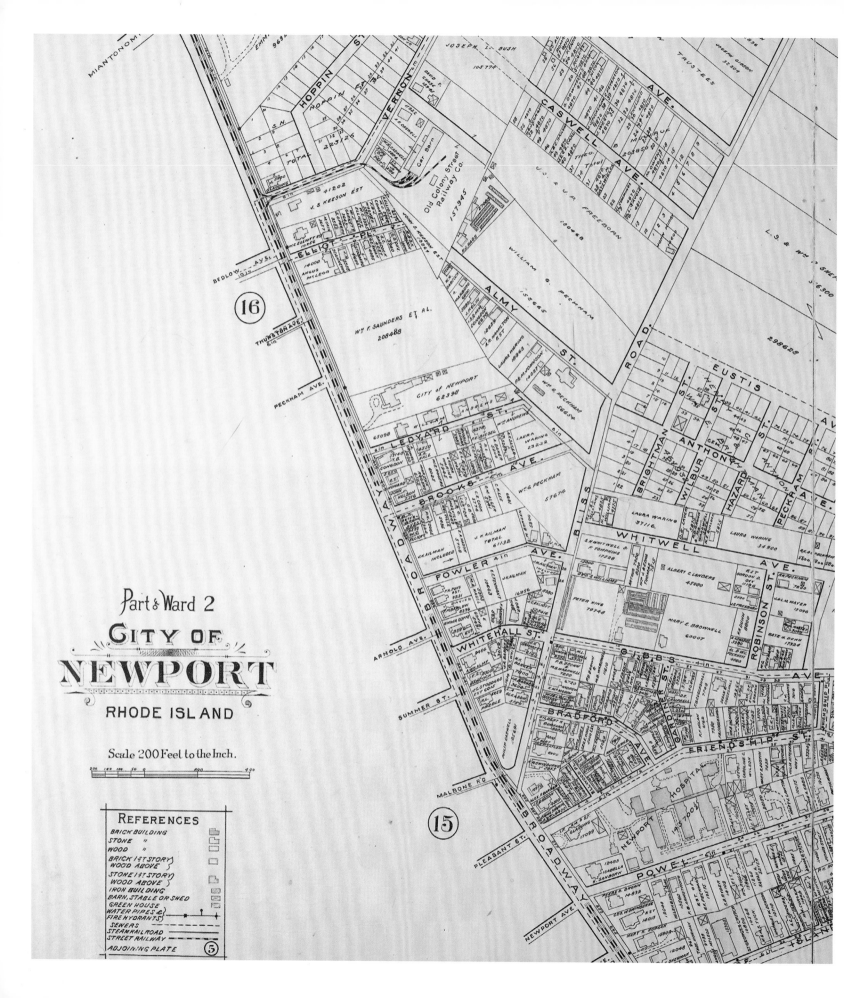

Part of Ward 2

CITY OF NEWPORT

RHODE ISLAND

Scale 200 Feet to the Inch.

REFERENCES

BRICK BUILDING
STONE "
WOOD "
BRICK 1ST STORY)
WOOD ABOVE)
STONE 1ST STORY)
WOOD ABOVE)
IRON BUILDING
BARN, STABLE OR SHED
GREEN HOUSE
WATER PIPES &
FIRE HYDRANTS
SEWERS
STEAM RAILROAD
STREET RAILWAY
ADJOINING PLATE
⑤

Fig. 183 *(previous page)*

L. J. Richards and Co., *Atlas of the City of Newport* (Springfield, MA, 1907). Newport Historical Society.

Broadway became the center of nineteenth-century civic buildings, including the City Hall and public schools.

Fig. 184

Newport City Hall, ca. 1890, photograph. Newport Historical Society, P17.

Fig. 185 (above)

The Bull House on Broadway, ca. 1885, photograph. Newport Historical Society, P9079.

This eighteenth-century house was demolished for the construction of the city hall.

Fig. 186 (right)

Newport City Hall hung in US flags and bunting, ca. 1915, photograph. Newport Historical Society, P2211.

Part & Ward 2
CITY OF
NEWPORT
RHODE ISLAND
Scale 200 Feet to the Inch.

Fig. 187

A map of the northern sector of Newport, from
L. J. Richards and Co., *Atlas of the City of Newport*
(Springfield, MA, 1907). Newport Historical Society.

The lands to the west (left) of West Main Road
remained either largely rural or the site of country
estates until the mid-twentieth century.

of Newport and traversed the length of Aquidneck
Island along both East and West Main Roads, linking
by bridge and ferry to Fall River, Massachusetts, and
Providence, Rhode Island.

While the southern portion of Broadway
developed as a residential district in the late
nineteenth century, the northern half, turning into
West Main Road and terminating at One Mile
Corner, remained largely rural (Fig. 187). To the
east of Broadway, in the hilly terrain overlooking
Easton's Pond and the fields of distant Middletown,

grand houses arose, such as the Greek Revival Elmhyrst (1835) (Fig. 188) and the Italianate Hamilton Hoppin House (1857), both designed by Richard Upjohn.[76] To the west, meadowlands were set against a slope that offered panoramic views of Narragansett Bay. This was the site of farms and country estates, such as the Gothic Revival–style Malbone (1849) (Fig. 189) by Alexander Jackson Davis. Both Davis and Upjohn were leading figures in American architecture at mid-century. Their work was published nationally and Upjohn, in 1857, became the first president of the American Institute of Architects. Thus, this northern portion of Newport claimed both architectural renown and pastoral beauty.

In 1921, the city acquired extensive acreage on a high point of land to the west of Broadway to create Miantonomi Memorial Park (Fig. 190), named in honor of a chief of the Narragansetts.[77] The appreciation of the historical associations of

Fig. 188 *(above left)*

Elmhyrst (1835), ca. 1920, photograph. Newport Historical Society, P5180.

Fig. 189 *(above right)*

Malbone (1849), ca. 1920, photograph. Newport Historical Society, P5832.

landscape and the preservation of open space that inspired the park's creation were exceptions. With the expansion of the US Navy during World War II and rapid residential and commercial growth in the mid-twentieth century, this area of Newport was radically altered. Its historical background had little or no influence on the plans of developers; its pastoral quality all but vanished in the face of development.

The US Naval War College occupied Coasters Harbor Island and the waterfront since the mid-1800s.

193

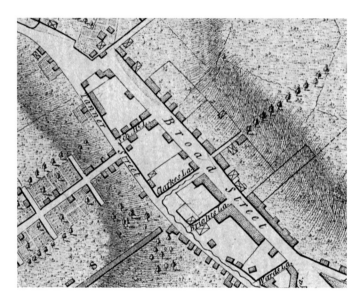

Fig. 190 *(left)*

The World War I Memorial Tower in Miantonomi Park, ca. 1930, photograph. Newport Historical Society, 2009.3.153.

Fig. 191 *(below)*

Charles Blaskowitz, *Plan of the Towne of Newport* (detail of Tanner Street), 1777. Library of Congress.

But during the 1940s, large parcels of land between Broadway and the bay were allocated as housing for naval personnel and defense workers at Park Holm and Tonomy Hill.[78] With the advent of automobile use in the post–World War II era, the commercial heart of Broadway decreased in value as shopping centers in nearby Middletown offered greater access and convenience in parking.

Abandoned, underutilized, and blighted buildings prompted the Newport Redevelopment Authority, founded in 1949, to state that West Broadway was the area most urgently in need.[79] The street has had

many iterations through the centuries. Originally, it was listed as Tanner Street on the Blaskowitz map of 1777 (Fig. 191); it was renamed West Broadway in the nineteenth century and remained so until urban renewal threatened its very existence. During the late 1940s, the Newport Redevelopment Authority focused its attentions on this specific street, citing the number of derelict and unoccupied buildings, allocating funds for the wholesale clearance of buildings. The removal of electric streetcar tracks on nearby Broadway was also listed as a priority. An entire system of buildings and a transportation network viewed as outmoded

Fig. 192 *(left)*

The Lawton Shop on West Broadway and Marlborough Street, ca. 1890, photograph. Newport Historical Society, P69.

Fig. 193 *(below)*

The demolition of the Lawton Shop on West Broadway and Marlborough Street, ca. 1935, photograph. Newport Historical Society, P8887.

was to be obliterated.[80] The streetcar tracks were pulled up and discarded, but the community at large resisted redevelopment efforts and, by 1958, the agency's plan for much of West Broadway had largely failed.[81] Buildings in the southern portion were demolished, but the northern half retained its Victorian era commercial and domestic structures.

By the 1960s, attentions had turned to the needs of downtown Newport, the site of earliest colonial settlement. Thus, the majority of buildings lining Broadway, dating from the mid-nineteenth to early twentieth centuries, have remained intact. The tension between the aims of the redevelopment authority and the residents of Broadway during the 1950s was a bellwether for a decade-long debate about different, and often polarizing, approaches to addressing urban decay (Figs. 192 and 193). The fate of Broadway was due, in great part, to the lack of interest in its historic or scenic merits. Few artists celebrated this area in prose, poetry, paint, or photography as in Washington Square, Historic Hill, or the Point. In 1994, however, the importance of history and historical figures was recognized on West Broadway, renamed Dr. Marcus Wheatland

Fig. 194 *(below)*

Dr. Marcus Wheatland, ca. 1915, photograph. Newport Historical Society, P9321.

Dr. Wheatland was a prominent physician in Newport during the late nineteenth and early twentieth centuries.

Boulevard in honor of the leading African American physician who lived and practiced in Newport in the late nineteenth and early twentieth centuries (Fig. 194).

Construction of Newport Bridge between 1966 and 1969 had a major impact on Newport and, specifically, the northern end of the city. Proponents began to advocate for a bridge linking Aquidneck Island and Jamestown as early as 1935 and the debate raged for over thirty years.[82] During the design process, nine proposed locations for the

Fig. 195

Construction of the access road for Newport Bridge, 1967, photograph. John T. Hopf Collection, Newport Historical Society, P8386.

To the south (left) is the historic district of the Point, rich in eighteenth-century architecture. To the north and east (foreground and right), the open farmland provided space for the access road to Newport Bridge. The location of the road was the impetus for further commercial development of remaining open space in the northern sector of Newport.

Fig. 196

Newport Bridge, 1970, photograph, *Newport Daily News.* John T. Hopf Collection, Newport Historical Society, P6640.

bridge terminus caused major concerns. The list of proposals caused shock or approval, depending on one's perspective. One scenario had the bridge link to Fort Adams; one cut through the historic Point neighborhood; four connected the bridge to downtown Newport; and three placed the terminus in Middletown (Figs. 195 and 196).[83] To avoid disrupting historic streets and buildings, the main point of entry and exit occurred at the northern border of the Point on open land near the US Naval Hospital. Officially opened on June 28, 1969, the Newport Bridge resulted in a completely new function for the northern end of the city. Remaining open land became commercially viable. The age of summer estates, farms, and open meadowlands was relegated to the past. There was initially no grand plan for redevelopment or historic restoration for the

buildings in and around Broadway, but the historic integrity of the area was appreciated by many of its residents, whose beliefs were expressed in the Rhode Island State Preservation Survey of 1977.

> *The West Broadway neighborhood retains physical traces of all periods in Newport's development. Each residential area and commercial district played its part in the growth and expansion of the city's civic, social and economic life.*[84]

Aware of the inherent value of the district, both community and individual efforts produced remarkable results at revitalizing Broadway from the 1970s to the present. The cityscape that once worked so well as a retail district was revived with stores, restaurants, and shops inhabiting structures built for these purposes.

George H. Norman and Newport's Urban Infrastructure

EILEEN WARBURTON, PhD

GEORGE H. NORMAN WAS A TRANSFORMATIONAL character in Newport's evolution. When he was born, Newport was an old-fashioned seaport, historically important, but isolated at the tip of Aquidneck Island. Through his vision, ambition, and creative engineering, Norman left Newport an expanding and livable modern city with some of the most up-to-date infrastructure in the country.

Born on New Year's Day, 1827, on Washington Street on the Point, to a longtime Newport family of very modest means, George attended Newport public schools until he was fourteen. Classmates remembered him, even as a small child, as a curious, bright boy who loved to make things with his hands. By the end of his life they were calling him a "far-seeing" man with "a vigorous intellect."

By the time George was sixteen, he owned a shoe store at Thames Street and Ferry Wharf. When he was barely nineteen, he rallied four friends to start a daily local newspaper, the four of them putting their backs into turning an old handpress to print the first issue of the first edition of the *Newport Daily News* on May 4, 1846. By 1849, George and his pal Bill Cranston, who was also the mayor, were the sole publishers. Bill was the editor and George was the reporter, staff writer, editorial writer, advertising manager, and bookkeeper. The partners introduced the first steam-operated press in the state. The *Newport Daily News* remains Newport's newspaper of record today.

Running a daily newspaper was this insightful young man's firsthand education into how a city works and how the health of a growing community depends on modernizing the city's infrastructure. Norman became aware of how other American communities were expanding their urban services in transportation, street paving, and lighting, water, and sewage. When, in 1856, a Mr. Warrington

Marshall of Boston, George H. Norman, ca. 1890,
photograph. Newport Historical Society, P8928.

sought the newspaper's support in publicizing his project to bring gas into Newport to light streets and houses, Norman sold his interest in the newspaper to buy into the new venture and become Warrington's secretary. Within a year, he owned his own company, contracting on his own to build the gasworks for Bristol, Rhode Island.

Bristol was the preferred destination for wealthy summer visitors from Cuba, a group of whom approached Norman with a scheme for constructing gasworks between Santiago de Cuba and Havana. He traveled to Cuba and installed a plant in 1858, returning to Newport with his pockets literally filled with gold—fifty thousand dollars in gold coin. With his new wealth and success, he was able in 1859 to marry Abbie Durfee Kinsley, the only child of Rufus B. Kinsley, a wealthy and influential businessman in Newport, owner of an extensive New England network of overland shipping and postal delivery, and the founder of a Newport bank. George and Abbie Norman eventually established themselves at Belair, which, in the 1870s, was one of Newport's most beautiful estates. Their nine children grew up to distinguish themselves in business, public office, philanthropy, fashionable society, agriculture, banking, and early environmentalism.

Norman, who was entirely self-taught as an engineer, built only one more gasworks, at West Point, New York. He had become convinced that the transformational technology for American cities was urban waterworks. Providing clean water, along with the installation of efficient sanitation systems, was probably the key to the creation of modern cities. This was an era when newspapers regularly issued warnings, especially in hot weather, about the dangers of drinking polluted water from wells, rivers, and streams.

On April 7, 1888, the *Newport Daily News* published dire warnings about cities such as Albany, Chicago, Saint Louis, and Cincinnati, where, "the fever rages violently. ... Water is of very poor quality ..." and these cities "plagued with "cholera, typhoid, and malarial fevers."

Norman moved from constructing urban gasworks to building waterworks for cities all across the United States. Ultimately, he supplied more American cities with water than any other engineer of his day and generation. His first contract was Middletown, Connecticut. After that, he built waterworks for cities up and down New England and New York State, and as far west as Colorado and Wisconsin: in all, over forty-one cities.

199

Many who later wrote about George H. Norman were of the opinion that the challenge of building waterworks for cities suited George better than building gasworks. Backed by his own growing capital and his father-in-law's fortune and banking contacts, George was exceedingly bold in making contracts with various cities. When municipal authorities were nervous and hesitant, he readily took the risk and supplied the capital as well as his talent for the successful completion of the waterworks. The result was that he held a controlling interest in numerous municipal waterworks all around the country, and he was a millionaire many times over.

However, the water project nearest his heart was always Newport and he prepared for it for years before making his move. Norman was aware that Newport was poised to become a great summer resort, but would only attract wealthy visitors if the quality of the water was healthy and good. Little by little, he bought control of all land on Aquidneck Island that would be suitable in the future for impounding water. In dozens and dozens of tiny purchases, he bought up the headwaters of every brook, well, and spring on the island.

By 1876, when he was ready to begin, there were many people who vehemently opposed Norman's proposal for a privately developed city waterworks. Norman promised that he would ultimately turn control over to the city after developing the waterworks at his own expense. All he asked was that his company should receive the contract to lay all the pipes throughout the city and provide water to the city, tax-free for fifty years. He even used his considerable political clout to have the state's general assembly pass an act that authorized any town council in the state to grant to any individual or corporation the exclusive right to lay water pipes in any of the public highways of such town or city. The act also included the power and authority to exempt such pipes and the connected works from taxation. Shortly after, Norman was granted his contract by the Newport city council to construct a complete waterworks for the water supply of the city of Newport, upon the condition that the city council would grant Norman and his heirs the exclusive right of laying all water pipes in all the streets and roads of Newport for the term of fifty years, tax-free. He was also to be granted all rights to Easton's Pond and the surrounding marshlands, north of a line running parallel and fifty feet north of the center of the road crossing the beach. Construction began in 1878. Fifty years later, the city reclaimed the Newport Water Works from the Norman family by stock purchase and eminent domain.

For the next twenty years, while pipes were laid and homes and businesses connected to city water, Norman personally managed and directed the continual expansion and improvement of the waterworks. He was constantly tinkering with it, inventing, for example, the first gravity pressure filtration system in 1888. By 1900, the Newport Water Works encompassed the south and north ponds of Easton's Pond, both enlarged by reclaiming the marsh and raising dams and berms. Supplementary works were created at Paradise in Middletown with both Gardiner Pond and Nelson

Newport Water Works employees, ca. 1900, photograph. Newport Historical Society, P4303.

Located on Marlborough Street, the Water Works were demolished in the late 1960s as part of urban renewal.

Pond dredged and surrounded with a berm and the construction of a storage pond in Portsmouth west of Union Street. A modern filtering plant was installed near the pumping station. When George died on February 4, 1900, work was just beginning to drain the large area near Lawton's Valley to construct another storage reservoir.

A commitment to and deep understanding of civic life motivated George H. Norman. Locally, he sat on numerous boards and organizations and was invested in many businesses. He was one of Newport's great philanthropists, donating especially generously to the public schools and to libraries, both public and private. He never ran for public office, but he was a lifelong Republican who was deeply interested in national affairs. He was twice a presidential elector for Rhode Island. Two of his sons served in Rhode Island government. Five of the six Norman sons served on active duty in the Spanish-American War.

These same six sons would carry George H. Norman's casket into Trinity Church for his February 1900 funeral, which jammed the streets of Newport with mourning admirers from near and far, stopping traffic, closing city businesses, and lowering flags. On February 5, 1900, the *Boston Post* reported, "Newport has lost her most energetic and progressive citizen."

CHAPTER 5

ROMANTIC VIEWS

Artists, Writers, and Mythic Visions of Newport

NEWPORT LENDS ITSELF TO ROMANTIC VIEWS. The spectacular natural scenery and the layered history of its streets, rich in the architecture of the past and distilling the memories of historical events, were, and still are, a natural draw for those involved in media from architecture and painting to poetry, prose, and photography. While each artist brought his or her specific interests and viewpoints, they collectively acted as the mythmakers of Newport. Their work during the nineteenth and twentieth centuries was a critical aspect of the emerging recognition of the city as a historic place of national significance.

Opposite

A. Gergner, The artist Edward Mitchell Bannister and companions at Battery Park on the Point, ca. 1887, photograph. Newport Historical Society, P39.

Dwelling on the past through its remaining buildings and sites, both grand and modest, preoccupied many a nineteenth-century artist; foremost among them in the United States was the poet Henry Wadsworth Longfellow, who visited the Jewish cemetery at Newport in 1852. Located at the northern point of Jew Street, which in 1853 was incorporated into the expanded and newly laid out Bellevue Avenue, the cemetery's main entrance gate was designed by Isaiah Rogers in the form of an ancient Egyptian pylon (ca. 1843), while obelisks served as posts for the surrounding cast-iron fence. Longfellow published his musings on the cemetery as an elegy to the community of Sephardic Jews from Portugal who had settled in Newport in the mid-1600s. He regarded the site as eliciting thoughts not only of this group who once dwelled in a seaside town, but evoking the centuries-old struggle of a people. His poem, "The Jewish Cemetery

Fig. 197

George Champlin Mason, State House and Parade, ca. 1870, lithograph. Newport Historical Society, 2004.13.49.

Mason, a Newport resident, artist, and promoter of the city's natural scenery and historic sites, created this romantic view of the center of town.

at Newport" (1854), is one of the earliest works inspired by a historic place in Newport's urban scene, and its opening lines speak of both the past and present which struck the author with such force.

How strange it seems! These Hebrews in
their graves,
Close by the street of this fair seaport town,
Silent beside the never-silent waves,
At rest in all of this up and down![85]

Emma Lazarus, a prominent poet and summer resident of Newport, responded to Longfellow with her own poem, "In the Jewish Synagogue at Newport" (1867), inspired by Touro Synagogue (1763). Descended from Sephardic Jews who had settled in New York City in the eighteenth century, Lazarus was drawn to the synagogue in Newport and its associations with her own heritage. Early in her writing career, at the age of eighteen, she used her verse to ponder a site of memory:

Here, where the noises of the busy town,
The ocean's plunge and roar can enter not,

We stand and gaze around with tearful awe,
And muse upon the consecrated spot.[86]

At the time both Longfellow and Lazarus wrote their respective poems, Touro Synagogue was generally closed, only being used for special services. The silence of the building resonated with both artists, the stillness powerfully evoking the past. Viewing the landmark as a witness to the centuries, Lazarus continued her poem with a reflection on time:

How we gaze, in this new world of light,
Upon this relic of the days of old,
The present vanishes, and tropic bloom
And Eastern towns and temples we behold.[87]

With the renowned American essayist and poet Ralph Waldo Emerson as her mentor, and with such British luminaries as Robert Browning and William Morris as friends and fellow poets, Emma Lazarus was a highly respected artist in her home country and abroad. In 1883, the lines "Give me your tired, your poor, / Your huddled masses yearning to breathe free" were among those from

Fig. 198

William James Stillman, The Bull House (1638), 1874, photograph. McKim Portfolio, Newport Historical Society, P391.

Charles Follen McKim took inspiration not only from his study of classical architecture in Europe, but from the wooden structures of Newport's colonial past. His 1874 commission of photographs of Newport's eighteenth-century buildings demonstrates his fascination for these vernacular structures. They served as design sources for his own architectural work in what was called the "modernized colonial" style.

Fig. 199

William James Stillman, Bridge Street, 1874, photograph. McKim Portfolio, Newport Historical Society, P392.

The scale and forms of Newport's colonial era streetscapes appealed to Charles Follen McKim.

her poem "The New Colossus" cast onto a bronze plaque for the Statue of Liberty. Emma Lazarus was one of many artists of national and international renown who responded to Newport's atmosphere resonating with history and infused with their own romantic imaginations.

Architects, writers, and painters followed poets in their attraction to Newport's famous landmarks, exploring the intimate scale and historic character of the old city. These admirers did not advocate for change; they venerated, extolled, and projected romantic views and ancient virtues on the place. The architect Charles Follen McKim, the third American to be educated at the École des Beaux-

Arts in Paris, saw the value of old cityscapes and buildings. He appreciated the classical tradition on display in Georgian doorways and in decorative details on houses in the Old Quarter and the Point. But he was drawn even more to the rambling rooflines and complex compositions of vernacular buildings; added to over time, they created picturesque ensembles on the wharves and in back gardens and alleyways (Figs. 198 and 199). In 1874, he commissioned a series of photographs to record Newport's eighteenth-century artistic heritage.[88] These images were a source of forms, ornamentation, and massing for McKim's remodeling of eighteenth-century houses

Fig. 200

William James Stillman, The Vernon House (ca. 1750), 1874, photograph. McKim Portfolio, Newport Historical Society, P384.

This photograph is rare due to its subject, a high-style Georgian house. Most of Stillman's work for the architect Charles Follen McKim consisted of views of vernacular buildings.

on the Point and his highly popular "modernized colonial" summer villas on Bellevue and Ochre Point Avenues throughout the 1870s and 1880s (Figs. 200–2).

McKim used the old in Newport to inform the new. Through his interests and efforts, and those of many other artists, Newport served as a powerful site of inspiration for the Colonial Revival style as the nation approached its centennial in 1876. What McKim sought in photographs and made into architecture, Henry James found with words, viewing Newport as a remnant of a mythic past. In 1906, he wrote of the city in a manner that highlights aspects of the colonial quarter—not to document the place, but to assertively evoke its mood:

What indeed but very old ladies did they resemble, the little very old streets … ? In this mild town corner, when it was so indicated that the grass should be growing between the primitive paving stones, and where indeed I honestly think it mainly is, whatever remains of them, ancient peace had appeared formerly to reign—though attended by the ghost of ancient war, inasmuch as these had indubitably been the haunts of our auxiliary French officers during the Revolution.[89]

The author imagined the inhabitants that lived in the streetscapes and buildings of Newport, inferring that images from long ago could appear to those who stopped, looked, and listened (Fig. 197). His

Fig. 201 (*opposite*)

William James Stillman, Detail of the door of the
Taylor House, 1874, photograph. McKim Portfolio,
Newport Historical Society, P395.

The exuberant carving of eighteenth-century houses
enlivened Newport's colonial streetscapes. These details
were integrated into the Colonial Revival work that
Charles Follen McKim produced for both eighteenth-
century houses he redesigned in Newport as well as
new villas on Bellevue and Ochre Point Avenues.

Fig. 202 (*above*)

William James Stillman, White Horse Tavern, 1874,
photograph. McKim Portfolio, Newport Historical
Society, P388.

writing imbued the urban scene with personality and
its own particular psychology of space and emotion.
For James, Newport morphed into both a place
and a person with distinct character traits. Nobility,
bravery, vanity, and gluttony are elicited by the
buildings, lanes, and landscapes encountered by the
writer on his literal and figurative wanderings.

The aesthetic view illustrated in James's writing
and the antiquarian interest exhibited by McKim's
photography mix easily in Childe Hassam's paintings
of Newport. This leading American impressionist used
the soaring steeple of Trinity Church (1726), a notable
landmark from the city's days as a powerful seaport,
in his work *White Church at Newport* of 1901.
With soft, dappled brushstrokes and gentle light, the

he old ewport and the new

T N

artist renders the white steeple among the cluster of buildings, lush trees, and gardens. His is truly a hazy suggestion of the old church, imbued with the optical experiments inherent in impressionist works of the time. He made an iconic image, calling upon history to confer gravitas to his work while executing it in the current painting techniques of the day.

At the dawn of the twentieth century, the juxtaposition of old and new in Newport, so clearly expressed in Hassam's painting, became even more striking. Linked to the mainland by train and steamship, Newport no longer functioned as

Fig. 203 a & b

Raymond Crawford Ewer, "A Sketch-Book at Newport: What a Puck Artist Saw at Society's Summer Capital," (detail) *Puck Magazine* 75, no. 1949 (July 11, 1914). Library of Congress.

Ewer produced a sketch of Newport rare in its inclusion of fashionable society and the decaying colonial districts of the waterfront on Thames Street. Like many artists, the creator of this sketch captures the architecturally complex and layered streets of the city.

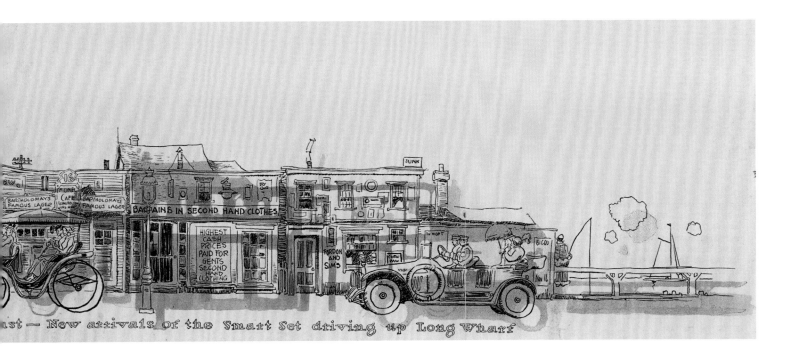

st — New arrivals of the Smart Set driving up Long Wharf

an isolated coastal port. The old quarter became increasingly appreciated for its associations with the colonial past, while the Victorian resort of wooden cottages gave way to a gilded Newport in its ascendancy (Fig. 203). With each passing decade, the character of this urban scene called to the next generation of artists, specifically Thornton Wilder. Combining a razor-sharp observation of the contemporary city with romantic longing, Wilder portrayed Newport as a rich composition of historical and cultural layers akin to ancient Troy. There, the renowned archaeologist Heinrich Schliemann took decades to sift through seemingly endless substrata of settlements in order to unearth the actual city, once home to the legends of the *Iliad*. In *Theophilus North*, set in 1926, Wilder's young hero is introduced to the nine cities of Newport, where he—in the role of archaeologist, anthropologist, historian, and explorer—investigates a myriad of built environments and their human inhabitants (Fig. 204):

The FIRST CITY exhibits the vestiges of the earliest settlers containing the enigmatic Stone Tower. ... The SECOND CITY is the splendid 18th century town with memories of Washington, Rochambeau and Revolutionary glory. ... The THIRD CITY contains what remain of a prosperous seaport along the wharves and docks of Thames Street. ... The FOURTH CITY belongs to the Army and Navy. ... The FIFTH CITY was inhabited since the early 19th century by intellectuals and artists. ... The SIXTH CITY is for the very rich, the empire builders, a place for fashion and competitive display; The SEVENTH CITY swarms with armies of servants. ... The EIGHTH CITY of parasites is dependent on the rich, filled with fortune-hunters, aspirants to social prominence, and prying journalists. ... The NINTH CITY is a middle class town, busy with its own life and taking little notice of the other eight cities.[90]

Wilder distills the social and physical nuances of Newport in a period before economic depression and World War II. Drawn to the city's historic atmosphere and natural charms, like so many before him, Wilder writes a novel replete with his ability to infuse his story lines with a tender humanity: as characters walk the streets and live out their ambitions, fears, and hopes amid centuries-old buildings. Wilder wrote *Theophilus North* in 1973. Thus, it was already for him a place of memory as he recalled various Newport scenes and created heroes, heroines, villains, and all of the assorted inspiring and imperfect types in between with the benefit of hindsight.

Captivated by the ancient atmosphere of the town, Longfellow, Lazarus, McKim, James, Hassam, and Wilder, among others, explored and recast Newport in written, photographic, painted, and built form. Their sources of inspiration, whether colonial dwellings and cobbled streets, timeworn wharves, or the avenues and mansions of the rich and fashionable, served as places of memory where the past and present inform one another. The architecture, streetscapes, and scenery composing Newport's urban geography often served as their muse and, sometimes, as main characters in their work. Architects, painters, and writers drew inspiration from the faded buildings of the old quarter and waxed poetic about both a real and imagined past, but their work was not merely the musings of a romantic few. Their words and images had an impact on the future. The twentieth century brought the convulsive changes of demolition and

Fig. 204 *(opposite)*

Map of lower Thames Street and Bellevue Avenue, from L. J. Richards and Co., *Atlas of the City of Newport* (Springfield, MA, 1907). Newport Historical Society.

Thornton Wilder's description of the many cities of Newport is illustrated in this atlas map, which depicts the close proximity of the working waterfront of Thames Street, with its wharves and small house lots, and the fashionable villas of Bellevue Avenue, set in expansive lawns.

redevelopment to the colonial district, but the literary, antiquarian, and painterly passions of nineteenth- and twentieth-century artists established the historic and cultural value of Washington Square, Thames Street, and the Historic Hill. Mythmaking can exhibit great power and influence. Many a fine landmark and modest house would be saved because of the written and visual legacy of a handful of aesthetes and devotees of Newport's history and architectural remnants. Romantic views conjured up by generations of artists had a direct effect on reality, drawing attention to the city's landmarks and thoroughfares and establishing their historical and cultural significance, which, in turn, aided in their survival and preservation.

CHAPTER 6

MODERNISM MEETS HISTORIC PRESERVATION

Decay and development in mid-twentieth-century Newport spurred two movements: historic preservation and urban renewal. Both had the same objective in mind, to save the city. Both had different visions of how it should be implemented. Groups of concerned citizens formed the Preservation Society of Newport County in 1945 and Operation Clapboard in 1965. These private initiatives focused on the aesthetic and historic significance of individual buildings with the aim of preserving the eighteenth-century quarter. The Newport Redevelopment Authority, established by the city's representative council in December 1949,

Opposite

Demolitions in the area near the Brick Market, the sole survivor of urban renewal, ca. 1966, photograph. Newport Historical Society, P1204.

focused on assessing physical assets and addressing economic and social challenges. These and many other organizations and citizens would participate in what can only be described as both a dance and a boxing match. Sometimes they worked together, oftentimes not. This situation repeated itself in numerous cities across the nation, where history and renewal often worked at cross-purposes.

Newport greeted the twentieth century in an ambivalent fashion. The Great Depression and World War II changed the social and economic dynamics of the nation. The rise of modernism in architecture and urban planning dealt a death blow to the historicism and romanticism that underpinned the character of Newport's urban geography. Increasing physical decay marred the colonial quarter. The nineteenth-century summer villas were viewed by many as relics of an architectural methodology debased by excessive

Fig. 205

Duke Street looking north toward Marlborough Street, ca. 1900, photograph. Newport Historical Society, P82.

historic ornament. Taste, in a place for centuries at the forefront of fashion, had seemed to turn its back on Newport. Modernist principles of social and architectural regeneration struck at the heart of the city as an entity in need of major redesign. Urban renewal and preservation became two approaches to revitalizing Newport, both with the mission to save the city, but with very different approaches.

Isolated at the tip of Aquidneck Island, time might have passed by Newport except for the arrival of the automobile. Since the 1860s, travelers approached the city by train or ferry, with only the Stone Bridge in the northeastern corner of the island connecting Portsmouth with the mainland at Tiverton. The opening of Mount Hope Bridge in 1927 allowed for increased automobile traffic from Bristol and points north to Portsmouth. With the advent of World War II, Newport became the primary naval base for the North Atlantic Fleet with new demands for more housing and services. The eighteenth-century quarter went into a slow economic decline while the summer

houses of Bellevue Avenue and Ocean Drive, while many still occupied, never returned to their prewar opulence. With the conclusion of World War II, Newport's historic core offered more urban problems than promises. The age of urban renewal had arrived to offer, in the minds of its proponents, modern cities for a modern age.

Clearance of districts identified as "slums" became one of the most controversial aspects of urban revitalization from the 1940s through the 1960s (Fig. 205). Across the country, highways cutting through the center of cities and demolition of historic buildings proceeded at a steady pace until 1960, when a group of citizens protested plans for the clearance of large tracts of Greenwich Village in New York City to accommodate a new expressway. The journalist Jane Jacobs, a resident of Greenwich Village, joined the protest. In 1961, she published *The Death and Life of Great American Cities*, in which she outlined the vibrant social and cultural life of neighborhoods labeled as slums merely because of

Fig. 206

Cartoon, *Providence Journal*,
November 12, 1951.

The triumph of modernism, with its
emphasis on minimalist design and the
primacy of the car and the freeway,
is celebrated in this cartoon. Progress
and efficiency were the watchwords
of those advocating for the ideals of
modernism in urban planning during
the mid-twentieth century.

their outward appearance.[91] Jacobs also emphasized
the human scale of historic streetscapes and the need
for neighborhoods that foster human interaction,
both features of established urban centers that faced
obliteration by urban renewal.[92] Through community
organization and the impact of Jane Jacobs's book,
Greenwich Village was preserved; its streetscape,
established in the early 1800s, remained intact.
Jacobs argued that city planners, in an attempt to
confront the challenges of urban decay, devised an
extreme solution of destroying healthy as well as
unhealthy parts of a city.

While Jacobs's writings sparked national
awareness of the importance of historic preservation,
another author, Rachel Carson, took a similar
approach to the conservation and protection of
nature. In *Silent Spring*, published in 1962, Carson
outlined the deadly effect of the chemical DDT.
Intended to eradicate diseases and various problems
borne by mosquitoes and other insects, DDT also
killed beneficial flora and fauna. Both Jacobs and
Carson took a holistic approach, rooted in the
scientific observation of measurable data, to address
issues facing built and natural environments.
Their work was critical in raising awareness and
energizing the preservation and environmental
movements, which culminated in the passage of
the National Historic Preservation Act in 1966 and
the establishment of the Environmental Protection
Agency in 1970. Both of these federal actions
redirected and empowered the conflicts that would
arise in the shaping of historic urban centers—
especially in Newport, where architecture and nature
were the primary assets of the city.

Advocates for historic preservation, on the one
hand, and urban renewal, on the other, in Newport
were fueled by vocations to direct or protect their
vision of the city. Preservationists based their work
on seeing the architectural significance and beauty
beneath the decay of historic areas. Planners for
urban renewal scenarios promoted modern, light-
filled cities with improved traffic conditions and

public amenities (Fig. 206). The clash between these two groups centered on building demolition and new roads and played out in the local press. The *Newport Daily News*, reporting on the suggestions of a city planning technician in "Slum Clearance Steps Suggested," wrote, "Edwards' testimony dealt chiefly with inadequate streets and congestion. He said there was good housing but most of it was old."[93] The use of the word "old" inferred lesser value. The founders and supporters of the Preservation Society of Newport County had different opinions of housing described as "old." They commissioned an inventory of historic structures by Antoinette Downing, who focused on the eighteenth-century quarter, and Vincent J. Scully Jr., who worked on nineteenth- and early twentieth-century buildings. The study resulted in *The Architectural Heritage of Newport, Rhode Island, 1640–1915* (1952), a landmark publication raising awareness of the city's nationally significant buildings. Newport was found to have one of the largest collections of eighteenth-century wooden houses in North America, nineteenth-century Shingle-style architecture of exceptional quality, and Beaux-Arts summer houses by the nation's leading architects. The appendix included a plan for the restoration of Clarke Street, which proposed the demolition of all buildings after 1840. These later structures had filled in the once open gardens of the colonial era houses. Later additions to colonial era houses were to be removed, restoring the buildings to their original condition.[94] This plan was never implemented, but it reflected the tendency during the mid-twentieth century for preservationists to value one era over another. Even historic preservationists did, at times, wish to knock things down.

The evolving nature of historic preservation and its change in focus from individual buildings to entire historic districts came to the forefront in the 1960s. Newport's preservationists, focused on saving colonial architecture, were forced to confront challenges to the nineteenth-century city. In 1960, the firm of Tunnard and Harris produced a report for the Preservation Society of Newport County. Their work reflected the latest philosophies on urban planning and historic preservation, reflecting back on Olmsted's improvement plan of 1913 (Fig. 207) and proposing even more far-reaching preservation action:

In preservation planning today, we must see beyond the boundaries of all Newport to include the great 19th century estates and the rocky coastline of the Island's tip. Times have changed since Olmsted could point to the 'ostentatious' side of Newport—a new generation sees these 'palaces' of the early captains of industry artifacts eminently worth saving. … To preserve these as part of a plan for present day living, education and institutional uses almost as important as preservation planning is to the colonial seaport … the conservation of natural scenery is also vital. Olmsted's suggestions for Almy's Pond went unheeded; now the very coastline—Newport's incomparable rocky shore—is threatened by spot development.[95]

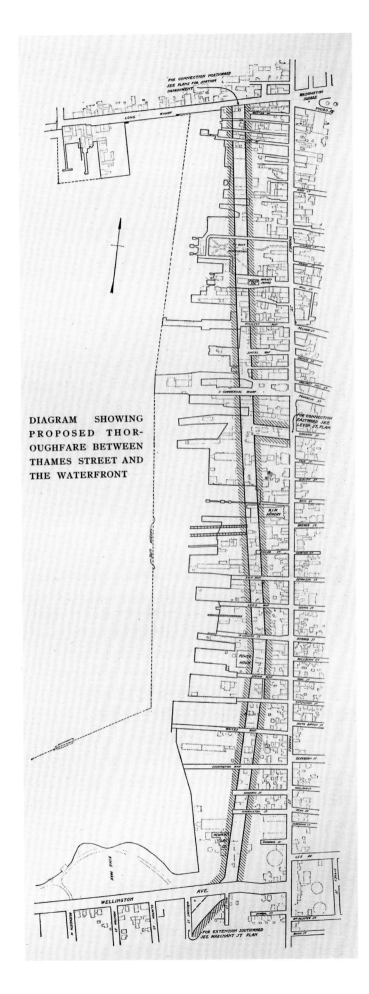

DIAGRAM SHOWING PROPOSED THOROUGHFARE BETWEEN THAMES STREET AND THE WATERFRONT

Fig. 207

Frederick Law Olmsted Jr., *Proposed Improvements for Newport*, 1913. Newport Historical Society.

The Olmsted plan provided a design for a new waterfront road to address increased traffic congestion. This idea for more efficient transportation in Newport led to a fifty-year debate on how to adapt the historic city core to modern needs. Eventually, America's Cup Avenue was created during urban renewal in the late 1960s.

Integrating landscape, buildings, and urban planning in one harmonious preservation scheme was visionary, a testament to Tunnard and Harris's sensitivities to nature and human-made structures. Their warnings were prophetic. Shortly after the completion of their report, a new challenge confronted Newport.

In the mid-1960s, the Newport Redevelopment Authority and the Rhode Island Turnpike and Bridge Authority both launched projects, decades in the making, that would have significant repercussions on the historic fabric of the city. The proposals for a Newport Bridge terminus in the heart of downtown and the creation of the four-lane America's Cup Avenue along the waterfront caused major concern. Nadine Pepys, founder and president of Operation Clapboard, a private organization dedicated to the revival of moribund neighborhoods, wrote to Governor Lincoln Chafee regarding the effects of these planning efforts as,

harmful to the historic heritage of Newport and will destroy much of its scenic beauty without providing much improvement other than wide roads and large areas of black topped car parks. ... Roads alone will not bring the tourist into Newport. Nor will they attract the

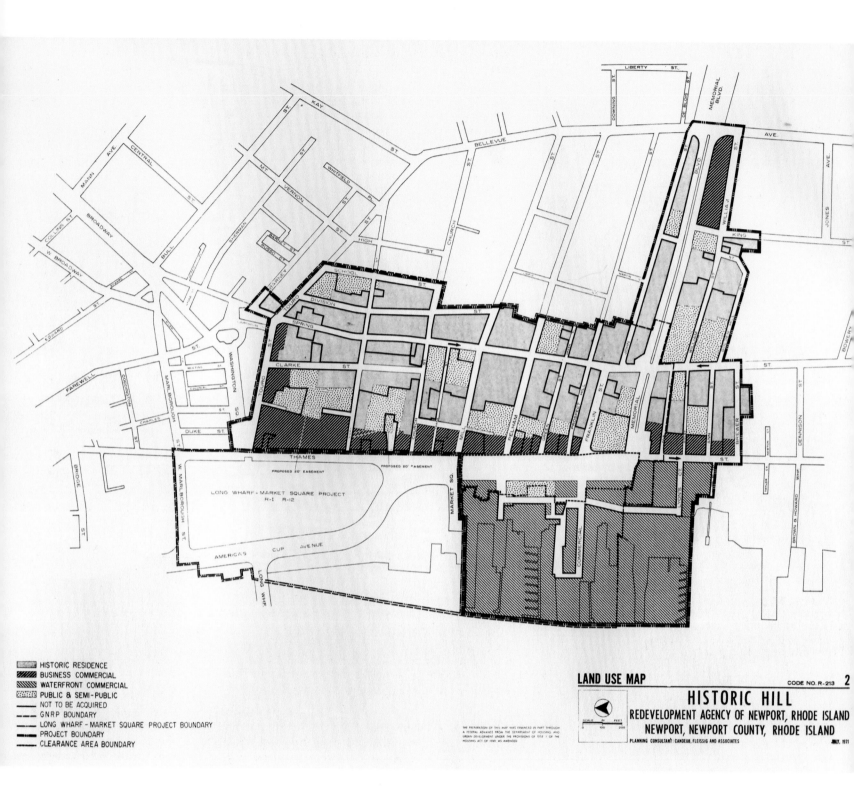

HISTORIC RESIDENCE
BUSINESS COMMERCIAL
WATERFRONT COMMERCIAL
PUBLIC & SEMI-PUBLIC
NOT TO BE ACQUIRED
GNRP BOUNDARY
LONG WHARF - MARKET SQUARE PROJECT BOUNDARY
PROJECT BOUNDARY
CLEARANCE AREA BOUNDARY

LAND USE MAP
CODE NO. R-213
2

HISTORIC HILL
REDEVELOPMENT AGENCY OF NEWPORT, RHODE ISLAND
NEWPORT, NEWPORT COUNTY, RHODE ISLAND
PLANNING CONSULTANT: CANDEUB, FLEISSIG AND ASSOCIATES
JULY, 1971

THE PREPARATION OF THIS MAP WAS FINANCED IN PART THROUGH
A FEDERAL ADVANCE FROM THE DEPARTMENT OF HOUSING AND
URBAN DEVELOPMENT UNDER THE PROVISIONS OF TITLE I OF THE
HOUSING ACT OF 1949, AS AMENDED

SCALE IN FEET
0   100   200

Fig. 208 *(opposite)*

The Urban Design Plan Historic Hill, Newport, Rhode Island, 1971. City of Newport.

The redevelopment plan for Thames Street/America's Cup Avenue, prepared for the city of Newport and the Newport Redevelopment Authority in the mid-1960s by the firm of Izadore, Candeub, Fleissig and Adly Associates. This scheme incorporates the meeting of the Newport Historic District, the protected area of buildings and streets outlined in a dark black line, with the redevelopment zone of the waterfront.

homeowner or the yachtsman, the student or the craftsman. Newport's greatest industry lies in its rich architectural heritage, and Operation Clapboard has shown in the few months since its inception, that this very heritage can, and is now, bringing into Newport new people and new money, to say nothing of new work.[96]

The impending demolitions in the colonial quarter and the near destruction of The Elms prompted a major effort to establish a historic district ordinance. After three years of campaigning by several organizations and citizens, the city declared by ordinance, in January 1965, the creation of the Newport Historic District and a Historic District Commission.[97] Just as this preservation victory was being celebrated, the greatest upheaval to the cityscape was about to take place. In the same year, 1965, the city council adopted an urban renewal plan developed by the Boston firm of Izadore, Candeub,

Fleissig and Adly Associates, which included a four-lane highway along the waterfront that would come to be known as America's Cup Avenue.[98] The newly established Newport Historic District did not include the waterfront (Fig. 208). As a result, the land was open for redevelopment. Historic preservation and urban renewal now had to exist side by side.

In 1966, urban renewal received federal funding, ensuring the completion of America's Cup Avenue. The *Newport Daily News* reported, "The year 1966, the Newport area was marked principally by condemnation of property, demolition of buildings, digging up of streets, all conversely leading to an anticipated healthy and prosperous future."[99] Newspapers published daily accounts on the monumental work of urban redevelopment and the preservationists' calls for protection of historic structures. Most of the eighteenth- and nineteenth-century commercial waterfront buildings from Long Wharf to the Perry Mill on Thames Street were cleared (Figs. 209–13). One writer proclaimed, "Newport searched for reasons … for the disappointment which had dropped on its waterfront redevelopment project with the force of a wrecking ball."[100]

The streetscapes of colonial era houses throughout the Hill and Point neighborhoods did present a remarkable preservation challenge and opportunity. These relatively compact buildings were not well suited for museum or commercial use and they were in areas of severe blight. The original colonial era streets also presented problems as reported by Tunnard and Harris:

Fig. 209 (top)

Urban renewal on Long Wharf, 1966, photograph. Rhode Island Collection, Providence Public Library, VM013_GF4756.

With the exception of the Brick Market, every building on Long Wharf was demolished for urban renewal. The Newport Water Works appears in the background, demolished during urban renewal.

Fig. 210 (middle)

Long Wharf demolitions, 1966, photograph. Rhode Island Collection, Providence Public Library, VM013_GF6279.

Fig. 211 (below)

Bowen's Wharf, ca. 1890, photograph. Newport Historical Society, P145.

This photograph depicts eighteenth- and nineteenth-century service buildings, later demolished during urban renewal of the late 1960s.

The Colony House and Brick Market, coming after the plan was set, make a focal point for Washington Square, but a square in name only. Instead, the town's important buildings are scattered, presently a most interesting urban scene, and, at the same time, a challenge to the ingenuity of those who are trying to preserve it … surroundings of commercial blight are the rule rather than the exception in Newport.[101]

The use of the word "blight" had negative implications for preservation, for it identified

Fig. 212 *(right)*

William James Stillman, The Wanton House (right) on Swan's Wharf, 1874, photograph. McKim Portfolio, Newport Historical Society, P387.

The architect Charles Follen McKim was intrigued by the formal architecture of the Wanton House (ca. 1750) and the surrounding vernacular buildings of the wharf. This area was demolished for urban renewal in the late 1960s.

Fig. 213 *(below)*

Demolitions for urban renewal in the old quarter, 1966, photograph. Rhode Island Collection, Providence Public Library, VM013_GF4757.

many vernacular nineteenth-century buildings as acceptable for demolition when, in fact, they formed a significant urban core (Figs. 214–18). Only landmark buildings and colonial period residences were deemed worthy of preservation (Figs. 219–21). The result of placing such a value system on what was to be preserved and the modernist emphasis on efficiency and access by automobile produced an environment where the original streetscapes were open to radical redesign. From 1966 to 1970, urban renewal produced the four-lane highway known as America's Cup Avenue, caused the destruction

Fig. 214 *(top left)*

The harbor from Thames Street, ca. 1940, photograph. Newport Historical Society, P139.

Fig. 215 *(above)*

The Thames Street waterfront, ca. 1960, photograph. Newport Historical Society, P9187.

Fig. 216

Trinity Church (1726) in the snow, ca. 1960, photograph. Newport Historical Society, P9583.

This aerial view captures the original setting of the church, positioned on a narrow lot between two streets: Church to the north (left) and Frank to the south (right). Trinity Church did not have a green common or urban square as a public frame for the structure. Buildings crowded around the base of the church, only the steeple standing tall in the skyline. Many schemes were proposed through the 1960s for a park in front of the church. Under the auspices of the Newport Restoration Foundation, the blocks in front of Trinity Church were cleared. Colonial era houses were moved for the creation of a park named Queen Anne Square.

Fig. 219 *(above left)*

Moving eighteenth-century houses, 1968, photograph. Newport Historical Society, P5684.

Fig. 220 *(above right)*

Pitts Head Tavern, ca. 1930, photograph. Newport Historical Society, P1869.

The tavern was moved from Washington Square to Charles Street, its location when this photograph was taken. In 1965, the building relocated to Bridge Street. Moving colonial era houses was one way of saving these structures from twentieth-century development or demolition.

Fig. 221 *(left)*

Pitts Head Tavern being moved from Charles Street to Bridge Street on the Point, 1965, photograph. Newport Historical Society, P9207.

Fig. 222

The Newport waterfront in the early twentieth century, from L. J. Richards and Co., *Atlas of the City of Newport* (Springfield, MA, 1907). Newport Historical Society.

Thames Street retained its historic density until urban renewal in the 1960s.

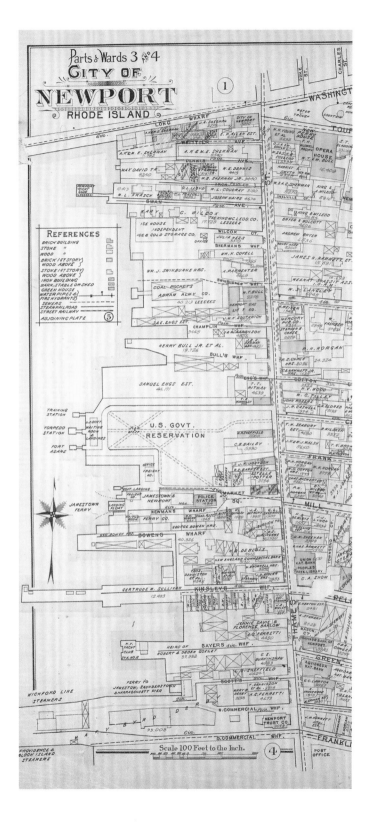

of the buildings on the west side of Thames Street from Church Street to Memorial Boulevard, created Perrotti Park on the harbor, and constructed new buildings on the wharves (Figs. 222–25). The extension of America's Cup Avenue into Memorial Boulevard precipitated the clearance of all buildings on Levin Street, eradicating whole blocks of historic buildings (Figs. 226–29). The greatest change was the reorientation of the east–west access of colonial side streets bringing pedestrians and traffic toward the harbor and wharves (Fig. 230). Instead, America's Cup Avenue severed that historic link with its north–south axis. This new orientation has been continually criticized: "its 98 foot width amputating the city functionally, visually and psychologically from the harbor that gave it birth."[102]

The construction of the Newport Bridge, from 1966 to 1969, also had a major impact on the city. The chairman of the Rhode Island Turnpike and Bridge Authority, Francis G. Dwyer, stated, "Newport's future is assured … it is in a position to compete with other areas in developing its tourist and recreation industry."[103] The Jamestown Ferry ceased operation with the opening of the Newport Bridge, ending hundreds of years of pedestrian traffic on the wharves. Progress prevailed in new roads, new buildings, and a new bridge, but the old still had its place, as so aptly expressed by journalist

Fig. 223 *(right)*

Maintaining Thames Street, ca. 1900, photograph. Newport Historical Society, P4222.

Workers are tending to the cobblestones on Thames Street. During the course of the twentieth century, Thames Street evolved from its colonial origins as a narrow, densely built urban core to an asphalt-paved thoroughfare. Some of the cobblestones survive in the northern sections of Thames Street.

Fig. 224 *(below)*

Infill for the embankment on the waterfront, 1968, photograph. John T. Hopf Collection, Newport Historical Society, P8076.

Eighteenth- and nineteenth-century wharves and buildings were demolished to create Perrotti Park.

Fig. 225 *(above)*

Long Wharf Mall, 1975, photograph. John T. Hopf Collection, Newport Historical Society, P8078.

This pedestrian mall replaced the street on part of the approach to Long Wharf, the end result of urban renewal.

Fig. 226 *(above)*

St. Mary's Church (right) and an eighteenth-century house (left) with Levin Street in the center, ca. 1900, photograph. Newport Historical Society, P5071.1.

The house and the dwellings on the north side of Levin Street (left) were demolished between 1966 and the early 1970s during the expansion of Memorial Boulevard, which linked America's Cup Avenue with Easton's Beach, creating a four-lane road through the center of Newport.

Fig. 227 *(above right)*

Colonial era houses on the north side of Levin Street, ca. 1940, photograph. Newport Historical Society, P9479.

These buildings were demolished in the late 1960s during the expansion of the street into Memorial Boulevard.

Brian C. Jones, who reported frequently on the entire redevelopment process: "Newport's unique collection of old buildings, having survived the Revolutionary War, now appear to be outlasting the 20th century urge to tear them down."[104]

The two often conflicting forces of urban renewal and preservation left their mark on the streets of Newport. Modern thoroughfares and historic buildings may have been at odds with one another, but they formed the basis of Newport's next incarnation as a place of major tourism, festivals, and leisure pursuits. In its three centuries of development, Newport had never been so radically altered as in the late 1960s, when it was directly linked to the mainland and the waterfront demolished for urban redevelopment. At the same time, preservation efforts rehabilitated whole sectors of the city. Both movements, one focused on preserving the old, the other on creating the new, produced a modern city renowned for a storied past with an architectural heritage.

Fig. 228 *(above)*

Levin Street, ca. 1935, photograph. Newport Historical Society, P9475.

The south side of Levin Street was preserved during the expansion into Memorial Boulevard.

Fig. 229 *(left)*

Streetcar in the snow, Levin Street, ca. 1920, photograph. Clarence Stanhope Collection, Newport Historical Society, P9552.

The electric railway streetcar system, introduced in Newport in 1889, connected Broadway, Spring Street, Levin Street, and Bath Road in one continuous route. This system was dismantled to accommodate motor vehicle traffic and the creation of America's Cup Avenue and Memorial Boulevard, which gave primacy to the car over public transport.

Fig. 230

America's Cup Avenue construction, 1968,
photograph. Newport Historical Society, P5319.

CONCLUSION
The Landmark City

THE STORY OF NEWPORT SINCE THE ESTABLISHMENT of the Newport Historic District in 1965 encompasses an increase in the number of private restorations, the opening of historic sites to the public, and a movement to safeguard the city's centuries-old tree canopy. History and preservation appear to be triumphant. Will history continue to determine the future of a place so revered for its storied past, architectural landmarks, and scenic beauty? The colonial town has been celebrated since the mid-nineteenth century and was the focus of attention during mid-twentieth-century preservation efforts, but the Victorian and Gilded Age districts came to the fore in the late 1960s. Newport celebrates its acknowledged position as a treasury of landmark buildings and districts to great effect. History is omnipresent. Some ages are heroic and define a city, but one cannot value only a certain celebrated age. The entire historical sweep and breadth of a city is best remembered, valued, and managed to allow for both preserved character and current innovation. The whole of Newport is the sum of all of its ages, which make it an accidental work of urban art of national significance.

Newport has experienced both the highs and lows of being a historic city. The articulation of what constituted a significant heritage and approaches to its maintenance formed the core of the Historic Hill urban renewal project survey and report of 1970. Antoinette Downing, chairwoman of the Rhode Island Historical Preservation and Heritage Commission, served as editor with a group of historians and planners. As the team assessed the district, their findings reflected a new approach to historic areas.

An interest in preserving not only single buildings but the total environment has increased, the impracticality of transforming cities into museum towns has become increasingly apparent ... the arbitrary designation of architectural and historic value to a specific period has been increasingly challenged and programs planned to restore an entire city to a single period (Williamsburg) cannot for contemporary concepts be justified.

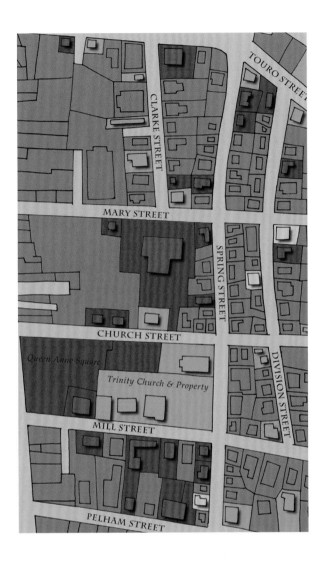

Fig. 231

Plan of the Queen Anne Square section of the Historic Hill, ca. 1970. Newport Restoration Foundation.

The properties in red indicate rehabilitation by the Newport Restoration Foundation. Orange areas are privately improved properties. Yellow indicates work by Operation Clapboard.

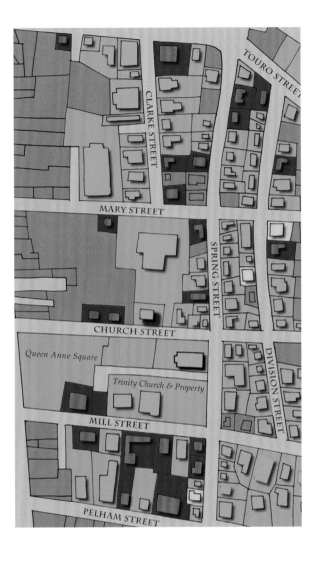

Fig. 232

Plan of the Queen Anne Square section of Historic Hill, 2010. Newport Restoration Foundation.

After nearly fifty years of work, the Newport Restoration Foundation's approach to urban revitalization through historic preservation produced remarkable results. The foundation's practice of restoring a critical mass of buildings served as an anchor for a district, prompting other private property owners to undertake their own preservation efforts. The sites in orange indicate these private preservation initiatives.

Removal of all later buildings falsifies history, freezing the town into a museum atmosphere and destroying the story of its evolving development ... except for the recent Memorial Boulevard construction and the demolition on the west side of Thames Street, the original street pattern established in the seventeenth and eighteenth centuries still remains ... drastic changes in the pattern of living in the twentieth century have already destroyed much of the environs and will engulf the older town unless specific plans to protect the remainder are put into effect.[105]

The report declared the importance of viewing Newport not only as a collection of a few time-honored structures, but as a complete urban entity. Thornton Wilder's interpretation of Newport as a place of many layers existed not only in fiction, but was a reality recognized by preservationists. During the course of the 1960s and 1970s, many of those neighborhoods immortalized as the "nine cities" in *Theophilus North* became officially sanctioned historic districts. In 1976, further recognition came with the National Park Service designation of the Newport Historic District, the Bellevue Avenue and Ochre Point Cliffs District, and the Ocean Drive District as National Historic Landmark Districts. History now looms large in most corners of the city. Heritage tourism has emerged as big business and preserved streetscapes, from an intimate colonial era lane to a leafy Victorian boulevard, are highly valued assets. Historic atmosphere is a prized commodity,

but how are past and present to be reconciled with the future?

The question of how to integrate historic preservation with a viable functioning urban center was given impetus in 1968 when Doris Duke created the Newport Restoration Foundation, dedicated to saving one house at a time. Doris Duke's vision was to rehabilitate Newport's colonial streetscapes without turning the city into a museum. Her foundation identified and acquired eighteenth-century houses, which were restored and leased to private occupants. The rehabilitation of one or two buildings on a block by the Newport Restoration Foundation spurred the repair of nearby structures by private individuals (Figs. 231 and 232). There is an identifiable style and finish to the houses restored under Doris Duke's efforts. They reflect a specific individual's approach backed up by research available at the time. Eventually, over eighty-five colonial houses were acquired by the foundation, maintaining both the buildings and, by extension, the historic character of the streetscapes of the Historic Hill and the Point.[106]

The area to the west of Trinity Church, in the 1960s a combination of historic structures and parking lots, was transformed by the Newport Restoration Foundation into Queen Anne Square, in fact an open green space much like town commons of the colonial era. Several planners had proposed a park for this site in the early 1960s, among them the firm of Tunnard and Harris, who envisioned an underground parking garage beneath their landscape plan. The Newport Restoration Foundation took this idea, absent the parking garage, and preserved the buildings from the area by moving them to different locations. While the scheme does not replicate the colonial cityscape of Newport, the area had lost much of its original fabric.

Every city has its challenges to preserving its historic character. Except for the demolition of the waterfront for America's Cup Avenue, the majority of Newport retains its centuries-old streets and cityscape. The urban plan, which evolved from the colonial era through the Victorian and Gilded Age periods, remains largely intact. Yet, the very nature of this city is based on a history of expansion, sometimes planned with a grand vision, oftentimes not. The urban historian Peter Hall writes of the role of such complexity and change in cities:

> So a very important part of living, and the creativity that comes out of it, has consisted in finding solutions to the city's own problems of order and organization … as cities grow in size and complexity, as their citizens define the good life in material terms, as they acquire the political power to insist on their right to that good life, so does the maintenance of urban order require a steadily greater sphere of collective action.[107]

Newport's urban history has been one of organic evolution and the debate over who is in charge of directing the physical form of streets, civic spaces, and architecture. The result, while never the product of a single grand plan, is a work of urban beauty and interest in its own right, distilling centuries of development. Nothing should be taken for granted in a city, not the past, present, nor the future. Newport may be viewed in many ways: as a work of art, as a place evoking various moods, and as a backdrop of the human condition. These are the components of a richly layered entity where beauty, age, and decay live side by side, as in the nine cities delineated by Thornton Wilder in *Theophilus North*. There are the indefinable qualities of Newport's streets, beyond the paving stones, the sidewalks, the fine old buildings, the overhanging trees, and the sea views. Elements both tangible and intangible make up a city that has been a cultural touchstone since its inception.

Newport is a repository of history and legend, where the dramatic topography and vistas of the sea remain omnipresent and buildings and streets still offer an architectural pageant of times past. For many, the reality of a historically intact streetscape gives weight to one's daydreams. Ideas are anchored in its buildings and streets, from the religious freedom and entrepreneurship of the colonial period, to the picturesque sentiments and technological advancements of the Victorian era, to the imperial aspirations of the Gilded Age, to the modernist hopes and preservationist victories of the twentieth century. Through all of these ages, Newport became an accidental work of urban art. Many forces drove the formation of the city, some incidental, some by design. It remains a place of memory, to be preserved, enriched, and interpreted. Most importantly and with difficulty, Newport must be allowed to evolve, for it is a cultural touchstone where ideas become real, where dreams are sought and fought over along its shores, in its buildings, and on its streets.

ENDNOTES

1 Wolfgang Braunfels, *Urban Design in Western Europe: Regime and Architecture, 900–1900* (Chicago: University of Chicago Press, 1961), 9–10.

2 Henry James, "The Sense of Newport," *Harper's Monthly Magazine*, August 1906, 344.

3 James, "Sense of Newport," 348.

4 Lawrence C. Wroth, *The Voyage of Giovanni da Verrazzano, 1524–1528* (New Haven, CT: Yale University Press, 1970), 133–34.

5 Records of the Colony of Rhode Island and Providence Plantations in New England, 1638–1644, C# 206, Folder 11/12, Rhode Island State Archives, Providence.

6 Deed for Aquidneck Island sold to William Coddington and followers by Narragansett Chief Sachem, Canonicus and Miantonomi, 1637, Rhode Island State Archives, Providence.

7 Antoinette Downing and Vincent J. Scully Jr., *The Architectural Heritage of Newport, Rhode Island, 1640–1915*, 2nd ed. (New York: Clarkson Potter, 1967), 15.

8 Records of the Colony of Rhode Island and Providence Plantations in New England, 1636–1663, C# 206, Folder 11/12, Rhode Island State Archives, Providence.

9 Records of the Colony of Rhode Island and Providence Plantations in New England, 1636–1663, C # 99, Rhode Island State Archives, Providence.

10 Rhode Island Land Evidences, vol. 1, 1648–1696, Rhode Island State Archives, Providence.

11 Rhode Island Land Evidences, vol. 1, 1648–1696, 16, Rhode Island State Archives, Providence.

12 Downing and Scully, *Architectural Heritage of Newport*, 17.

13 Downing and Scully, *Architectural Heritage of Newport*, 18.

14 Town Meeting Records, Newport Historical Society, 1:138. The town approved the paving of streets in 1707.

15 Downing and Scully, *Architectural Heritage of Newport*, 21.

16 Downing and Scully, *Architectural Heritage of Newport*, 54–55.

17 George Champlin Mason, *Annals of the Redwood Library* (Newport, RI: Redwood Library and Athenaeum, 1891), 12–13.

18 Veronica Biermann, Alexander Gronert, Christopher Jobst, and Roswitha Stewering, "Andrea Palladio," in *Architectural Theory from the Renaissance to the Present* (Cologne: TASCHEN, 2012), 110.

19 L. M. Friedman, "The Newport Synagogue," *Old Time New England* 36, no. 3 (January 1946): 49–57.

20 D. Scott Molloy, "Mass Transit in Rhode Island, Part 7," *The First Rhode Island Trolleys: Woonsocket and Newport, Old Rhode Island Magazine*, September 1994.

21 McKim Portfolio, Newport Historical Society.

22 James, "Sense of Newport," 351.

23 Frederick Law Olmsted, Jr., *Proposed Improvements for Newport*, 1913, 1.

24 Olmsted, *Proposed Improvements for Newport*, 6.

25 Charles A. Birnbaum and Robin Karson, *Pioneers of American Landscape Design* (New York: McGraw-Hill, 2000), 276–81.

26 There are seventy-six plans for the King, Glover, Bradley Platt, 1884–1885, Olmsted National Historic Site, Brookline, MA.

27 Arthur A. Shurtleff, *Regarding the Plans for the Growth of the City of Newport, R.I.* (January 20, 1926), 31.

28 Shurtleff, *Regarding the Plans for the Growth of the City of Newport*, 31.

29 Shurtleff, *Regarding the Plans for the Growth of the City of Newport*, 31–32.

30 "Waterfront Renewal," *Newport Daily News*, November 15, 1950.

31 Nicholas Easton, Last Will and Testament, 1674, Vault A, Box 82, Folder 6, Newport Historical Society. Ann Bull Easton deeded additional acreage on the Point to the Society of Friends in 1706. Ann Bull (Easton) Deed, Land Evidence, The Colony of Rhode Island and Providence Plantations, October 15, 1706, 360–62, Vault A, Box 82, Folder 6, Newport Historical Society.

32 Minutes of the Society of Friends, Newport, Rhode Island, Newport Historical Society.

33 Samuel Easton, Map of Easton's Point, 1725, Newport Historical Society.

34 Lewis Mumford, *The City in History* (New York: Harcourt, 1961), 192–93.

35 Leonardo Benevolo, *The History of the City* (Cambridge, MA: MIT Press, 1998), 639–41.

36 Molloy, "Mass Transit in Rhode Island."

37 L. J. Richards & Co., *Atlas of the City of Newport* (Springfield, MA, 1907), plate 3.

38 Thomas Wentworth Higginson, *Oldport Days* (Boston: James R. Osgood, 1873), 51–52.

39 Richard Guy Wilson, *McKim, Mead and White, Architects* (New York: Rizzoli, 1983), 53.

40 Higginson, *Oldport Days*, 17.

41 Hopkins, *City Atlas of Newport*, 78–79.

42 W. Mackenzie Woodward, "Draft: Ocean Drive National Historic Landmark Study," Rhode Island Historical and Preservation Commission, October 2008, Section 8, 5. In the mid-1840s, Alfred Smith developed three hundred acres of land in the Kay–Catherine–Old Beach Road area.

43 Woodward, "Draft: Ocean Drive," Section 8, 5.

44 G.M. Hopkins, *City Atlas of Newport, Rhode Island* (Philadelphia, 1876), 38–39.

45 G. Hayward, *Map of the Farm known as Easton Farm Situate at the Town Beach at Newport, RI belonging to the Estate of Mrs. Mary Gibbs, Dec..d.*, Surveyed by James Stevens (New York, 1845).

46 "Death of a Millionaire: Alfred Smith, Newport's Big Real Estate Agent, Dies Suddenly," *New York Times*, October 27, 1886, 8.

47 William Cullen Bryant, ed., "Newport," in *Picturesque America*, vol. 1 (New York: D. Appleton and Company, 1872), 362.

48 Andrew Jackson Downing, *The Architecture of Country Houses* (New York: Dover Publications, 1969), 113.

49 Downing, *Architecture of Country Houses*, 259.

50 William H. Jordy and Christopher Monkhouse, *Rhode Island Buildings on Paper: Rhode Island Architectural Drawings, 1825–1945* (Providence: Rhode Island School of Design,

Rhode Island Historical Society, and Bell Gallery, List Art Center, Brown University, 1982), 13–14.

51 Higginson, *Oldport Days*, 12–13.

52 Hopkins, *City Atlas of Newport*.

53 Woodward, "Draft: Ocean Drive," Section 8, 10.

54 Newport Land Evidence Records, September 9, 1863, Book 35, 313.

55 S. L. Minot, Map of Ocean Drive, also known as Shore Road, 1867, City Hall, Newport.

56 F. L. Olmsted, Jr. and J. C. Olmsted, "Plan for Subdivision of Properties in Newport, RI Belonging to Mrs. Edward King, Mr. J.H. Glover, Esq., The Hon. C.S. Bradley, G. Gordon King," Newport Land Evidence Office, Plat Book 1 (Newport, RI: Newport City Hall, 1884), 30–31.

57 Olmsted and Olmsted, "Plan for Subdivision of Properties," 31.

58 Mariana Griswold Van Rensselaer, "Newport-II," *Garden and Forest* 1 (December 5, 1888): 483.

59 "The Palace Cottages of Newport," *Munsey's Magazine*, September 1897.

60 Consuelo Vanderbilt Balsan, *The Glitter and the Gold* (New York: Random House, 1953), 52.

61 Barr Ferree, *American Estates and Gardens* (New York: Munn, 1904), 63–67.

62 James, "Sense of Newport," 346.

63 James, "Sense of Newport," 354.

64 James, "Sense of Newport," 354.

65 F. Lauriston Bullard, *Historic Summer Haunts from Newport to Portland* (Boston: Little, Brown, 1912), 1–3.

66 Molloy, "Mass Transit in Rhode Island."

67 Molloy, "Mass Transit in Rhode Island."

68 Rhode Island Historical Society, Mss 798, Boxes 14 and 15.

69 Rhode Island Historical Society, Mss 798, Box 15.

70 Rhode Island Historical Society, Mss 798, Letter of November 8, 1915.

71 "Bath Road Work Has Been Completed," *Newport Mercury*, July 7, 1933.

72 "Report on City Council Meeting," *Newport Mercury*, November 29, 1946.

73 "Life Visits a Fading Newport," *Life*, October 16, 1944.

74 Cleveland Amory, "The Crucial Battle for Modern Newport," *New York Times Magazine*, September 2, 1962.

75 Hopkins, *City Atlas of Newport*, 38–39.

76 Jordy and Monkhouse, *Rhode Island Buildings on Paper*, 12–13.

77 Tanya Kelly, *Cultural Landscapes Report on the City Parks of Newport, Rhode Island* (Newport, RI, 2018).

78 "Newport's Decade of Progress, 1940–1950," *Tenth Annual Report of the Housing Authority of the City of Newport, Rhode Island*, July 29, 1950. The report cited the completion of Park Holm in 1940 and Tonomy Hill in 1941 as examples of successful modernization efforts to provide affordable housing in Newport.

79 "Broadway," *Newport Daily News*, January 6, 1950.

80 "Newport's Decade of Progress, 1940–1950."

81 John F. A. Herzan, "The West Broadway Neighborhood in Newport, Rhode Island," State Historical Preservation Report N-N-2 (Providence: Rhode Island Historical Preservation Commission, 1977), 29.

82 James M. Ricci, *The Newport Bridge* (Charleston, SC: History Press, 2018), 44.

83 Ricci, *Newport Bridge*, 128.

84 Herzan, "West Broadway Neighborhood in Newport," 30.

85 Henry Wadsworth Longfellow, "The Jewish Cemetery at Newport," 1854.

86 Emma Lazarus, "In the Jewish Synagogue at Newport," 1867.

87 Lazarus, "In the Jewish Synagogue at Newport."

88 McKim Portfolio, Newport Historical Society.

89 James, "Sense of Newport," 351.

90 Thornton Wilder, *Theophilus North* (New York: Harper and Row, 1973), 15–16.

91 Jane Jacobs, *The Death and Life of Great American Cities* (New York: Random House, 1961).

92 Jacobs, *Death and Life of Great American Cities*, 87.

93 "Slum Clearance Steps Suggested," *Newport Daily News*, May 18, 1951.

94 Downing and Scully, *The Architectural Heritage of Newport*, 465–67.

95 Tunnard and Harris, *A Preservation Planning Report on Newport, Rhode Island*, January 1960, 2.

96 Letter from Nadine Pepys, president, Operation Clapboard, January 28, 1965, Chafee Papers. Ricci, *Newport Bridge*, 137.

97 Ordinance of the Council, No. 416, Chapter 149, January 27, 1965, City of Newport, Rhode Island.

98 "Council for the Renewal Plan," *Newport Daily News*, February 24, 1965.

99 "1966: The Pace Quickens in Newport," *Newport Daily News*, December 31, 1966.

100 "Amid the Rubble, Newport Asks Why," *Providence Journal*, April 21, 1968.

101 Tunnard and Harris, *Preservation Planning Report*, 2.

102 Taylor and Partners Town Center Team, "Plan 2004, Urban Design for Central Newport," October 20, 2004.

103 "Bridge Is Dedicated, Open to Traffic," *Newport Daily News*, June 28, 1969.

104 Brian C. Jones, "Tide Turns for Historic Newport," *Providence Journal*, March 31, 1968.

105 Antoinette Downing, ed., "Architectural Quality and History of the Buildings of the Historic Hill Urban Renewal Project, Newport, RI," Prepared for the Redevelopment Agency of Newport Under Contract with Oldport Association, October 1970, 2–4.

106 Robert Foley, A. Bruce Macleish, and Pieter Roos, *Extraordinary Vision: Doris Duke and the Newport Restoration Foundation* (Newport, RI: Newport Restoration Foundation, 2010), 18–19.

107 Peter Hall, *Cities in Civilization: Culture, Innovation and Urban Order* (London: Weidenfeld and Nicolson, 1998), 6.

BIBLIOGRAPHY

"Amid the Rubble, Newport Asks Why." *Providence Journal*, April 21, 1968.

Amory, Cleveland. "The Crucial Battle for Modern Newport." *New York Times Magazine*, September 2, 1962.

Atlas of Newport, Jamestown, Middletown and Portsmouth, RI. New York: Sanborn Map and Publishing, 1921.

Bacon, Edmund N. *Design of Cities*. New York: Penguin Books, 1967.

Balsan, Consuelo Vanderbilt. *The Glitter and the Gold*. New York: Random House, 1953.

"Bath Road Work Completed." *Newport Mercury*, July 7, 1933.

Benevolo, Leonardo. *The History of the City*. Cambridge, MA: MIT Press, 1998.

Biermann, Veronica, Alexander Gronert, Christopher Jobst, and Roswitha Stewering, "Andrea Palladio." In *Architectural Theory from the Renaissance to the Present*. Cologne: TASCHEN, 2012.

Birnbaum, Charles A., and Robin Karson. *Pioneers of American Landscape Design*. New York: McGraw-Hill, 2000.

"Board Votes to Call Bath Road Memorial Boulevard." *Newport Mercury*, November 29, 1946.

Bowditch, Ernest W. "The Year 1881 at the Office." *Office-Work Personalities II*, no. 10. Bowditch Family Papers. Salem: Essex Institute.

Braunfels, Wolfgang. *Urban Design in Western Europe: Regime and Architecture, 900–1900*. Chicago: University of Chicago Press, 1961.

"Bridge Is Dedicated, Open to Traffic." *Newport Daily News*, June 28, 1969.

Bryant, William Cullen, ed. "Newport." In *Picturesque America*, vol. I. New York: D. Appleton and Company, 1872.

Bullard, F. Lauriston. *Summer Haunts from Newport to Portland*. Boston: Little, Brown, 1912.

Carson, Rachel. *Silent Spring*. New York: Houghton Mifflin, 1962.

Collins, Holly. "The Preservation Society of Newport County 1945–1965, The Founding Years." Newport, RI: Preservation Society of Newport County, 2008.

Collins, Holly. "Rites of Passage: The Wetmores of Chateau-sur-Mer." Newport, RI: Preservation Society of Newport County, 2002.

"Council for the Renewal Plan." *Newport Daily News*, February 24, 1965.

"Death of a Millionaire: Alfred Smith, Newport's Big Real Estate Agent, Dies Suddenly." *New York Times*, October 27, 1886, 8.

Downing, Andrew Jackson. *The Architecture of Country Houses*. New York: Dover Publications, 1969.

Downing, Antoinette, ed. "Architectural Quality and History of the Buildings of the Historic Hill Urban Renewal Project, Newport, RI." Prepared for the Redevelopment Agency of Newport Under Contract with Oldport Association. October 1970.

Downing, Antoinette, and Vincent J. Scully Jr. *The Architectural Heritage of Newport, Rhode Island, 1640–1915*. 2nd ed. New York: Clarkson Potter, 1967.

Dripps, Matthew, and B. I. Tilley. *Map of the City of Newport*. New York and Newport, RI, 1859.

Easton, Nicholas. Last Will and Testament, 1674. Vault A, Box 82, Folder 6. Newport Historical Society.

Elliott, Maud Howe. *This Was My Newport*. Cambridge, MA: Mythology Company, 1944.

Ferree, Barr. *American Estates and Gardens*. New York: Munn, 1904.

Galt and Hoy. *Newport, RI*. New York, 1878.

Hall, Peter. *Cities in Civilization: Culture, Innovation and Urban Order*. London: Weidenfeld and Nicolson, 1998.

Hayward, G. *Map of the Farm known as Easton Farm Situate at the Town Beach at Newport, RI belonging to the Estate of Mrs. Mary Gibbs, Dec..d*. Surveyed by James Stevens. New York, 1845.

Herzan, John F. A. "The West Broadway Neighborhood in Newport, Rhode Island." State Historical Preservation Report N-N-2. Providence: Rhode Island Historical Preservation Commission, 1977.

Higginson, Thomas Wentworth. *Oldport Days*. Boston: James R. Osgood, 1873.

Hopkins, G. M. *City Atlas of Newport, Rhode Island*. Philadelphia, 1876.

Hopkins, G. M. *City Atlas of Newport, Rhode Island*. Philadelphia, 1883.

Hunter, Sam, ed. *Monumenta: A Biennial Exhibition of Outdoor Sculpture, Newport, Rhode Island, August 17 through October 13, 1974*. Newport, RI: Monumenta Newport, 1974.

Jacobs, Jane. *The Death and Life of Great American Cities*. New York: Random House, 1961.

James, Henry. "The Sense of Newport." *Harper's Monthly Magazine*, August 1906.

Jones, Brian C. "Tide Turns for Historic Newport." *Providence Journal*, March 31, 1968.

Jones, Daniel W., and James L. Yarnell. "Some Memories of Kittymouse." *Newport History: Journal of the Newport Historical Society* 81, no. 267 (Fall 2012): 1–41.

Kostof, Spiro. *The City Shaped: Urban Patterns and Meanings Through History*. New York: Bullfinch Press, 1991.

Kunstler, James Howard. *The Geography of Nowhere: The Rise and Decline of America's Man-Made Landscape*. New York: Simon and Schuster, 1993.

Lazarus, Emma. "In the Jewish Synagogue at Newport." 1867.

"Life Visits a Fading Newport." *Life*, October 16, 1944.

"Local Matters: Improvement Notes." *Newport Mercury*, March 9, 1889, 1.

"Local Matters: The New Road." *Newport Mercury*, May 4, 1867, 2.

"Local Matters: Ocean Avenue." *Newport Mercury*, October 19, 1867, 2.

"Local Matters: The Shore Road." *Newport Mercury*, May 11, 1867, 2.

Longfellow, Henry Wadsworth. "The Jewish Cemetery at Newport." 1854.

"Magnificent Newport." *Munsey's Magazine*, 1900.

Mason, George Champlin. *Annals of the Redwood Library*. Newport, RI: Redwood Library and Athenaeum, 1891.

Mason, George Champlin. Editorial. *Newport Mercury*, July 26, 1851, 2.

Mason, George Champlin. Editorial. *Newport Mercury*, October 17, 1857, 2.

Molloy, D. Scott. "Mass Transit in Rhode Island, Part 7." *The First Rhode Island Trolleys: Woonsocket and Newport. Old Rhode Island Magazine*, September 1994.

Mumford, Lewis. *The City in History*. New York: Harcourt, 1961.

National Register of Historic Places. Bellevue Avenue-Casino Historic District. Newport, Newport County, Rhode Island. National Register #72000024.

National Register of Historic Places. Newport Historic District. Newport, Newport County, Rhode Island. National Register #68000001.

National Register of Historic Places. Ocean Drive. Newport, Newport County, Rhode Island. National Register #76000048.

National Register of Historic Places. Ochre Point-Cliffs Historic District. Newport, Newport County, Rhode Island. National Register #75000211.

"Newport: The City by the Sea: Four Epochs in Her History." *Providence Daily Journal*, May 22, 1879, 5.

Newport, RI. New York: Sanborn Map and Publishing, 1884.

"Newport's Decade of Progress, 1940–1950." *Tenth Annual Report of the Housing Authority of the City of Newport, Rhode Island*. July 29, 1950.

"1966: The Pace Quickens in Newport." *Newport Daily News*, December 31, 1966.

"Obituary for George H. Norman." *Boston Post*, February 5, 1900.

Olmsted, F. L., and J. C. Olmsted. "Plan for Subdivision of Properties in Newport, RI Belonging to Mrs. Edward King, Mr. J.H. Glover, Esq., The Hon. C.S. Bradley, G. Gordon King." Newport Land Evidence Office, Plat Book 1. Newport, RI: Newport City Hall, 1884.

Olmsted, Frederick, Law Jr., *Proposed Improvements for Newport: A Report Prepared for the Newport Improvement Association*. 1913.

Ordinance of the Council, No. 416, Chapter 149. City of Newport, Rhode Island. January 27, 1965.

Records of the Colony of Rhode Island and Providence Plantations in New England, 1638–1644. C# 206, Folder 11/12. Rhode Island State Archives, Providence.

Representative Men and Old Families of Rhode Island: Genealogical Records and Historical Sketches of Prominent and Representative Citizens and of Many of the Old Families. Vol. 1. Chicago: J. H. Beers, 1908.

Rhode Island Historical Society. Mss 798, Box 16.

Rhode Island Land Evidences. Vol. 1, 1648–1696. Rhode Island State Archives, Providence.

Ricci, James M. *The Newport Bridge*. Charleston, SC: History Press, 2018.

Richards, L. J., and Co. *Atlas of the City of Newport*. Springfield, MA, 1893.

Richards, L. J., and Co. *Atlas of the City of Newport*. Springfield, MA, 1907.

Robinson, Jennifer, and James L. Yarnell. "Belair." *Newport History: Journal of the Newport Historical Society* 81, no. 267 (Fall 2012): 43–68.

"Rufus Kinsley Biggest Man in Newport in 1858." *Newport Daily News*, February 15, 1954.

Shurtleff, Arthur A. *Regarding the Plans for the Growth of the City of Newport, R.I.*, January 20, 1926.

"Slum Clearance Steps Suggested." *Newport Daily News*, May 18, 1951.

Society of Friends Records of Rhode Island Monthly Meetings, 1701–1739. Newport Historical Society.

Taylor and Partners Town Center Team. "Plan 2004, Urban Design for Central Newport," October 20, 2004.

"Tide Turns for Historic Newport." *Providence Journal*, March 31, 1968.

Tung, Anthony M. *Preserving the World's Great Cities*. New York: Clarkson Potter Publishers, 2001.

Tunnard and Harris. *A Preservation Planning Report on Newport, Rhode Island*. January 1960.

Van Rensselaer, Mariana Griswold. "American Country Dwellings." *Century Magazine*, May 1886.

Van Rensselaer, Mariana Griswold. "Newport-II." *Garden and Forest* 1 (December 5, 1888).

Waters, Henry Fitz-Gilbert. "George Henry Norman." In *The New England Historical and Genealogical Register*, edited by John Ward Dean, 55. Boston: New England Historic Genealogical Society, 1901.

Wilder, Thornton. *Theophilus North*. New York: Harper and Row, 1973.

Wilson, Richard Guy. *McKim, Mead and White, Architects*. New York: Rizzoli, 1983.

Woodward, W. Mackenzie. "Draft: Ocean Drive National Historic Landmark Study." Rhode Island Historical and Preservation Commission, October 2008.

Wroth, Lawrence C. *The Voyages of Giovanni da Verrazzano, 1524–1528*. New Haven, CT: Yale University Press, 1970.

INDEX

Scale 100 Feet to the Inch.